S. Hrg. 114–42

EMPOWERING INDIAN COUNTRY: COAL, JOBS, AND SELF-DETERMINATION

FIELD HEARING

BEFORE THE

COMMITTEE ON INDIAN AFFAIRS UNITED STATES SENATE

ONE HUNDRED FOURTEENTH CONGRESS

FIRST SESSION

APRIL 8, 2015

Printed for the use of the Committee on Indian Affairs

U.S. GOVERNMENT PUBLISHING OFFICE

95–500 PDF   WASHINGTON : 2015

For sale by the Superintendent of Documents, U.S. Government Publishing Office
Internet: bookstore.gpo.gov Phone: toll free (866) 512–1800; DC area (202) 512–1800
Fax: (202) 512–2104 Mail: Stop IDCC, Washington, DC 20402–0001

CONTENTS

EMPOWERING INDIAN COUNTRY: COAL, JOBS, AND SELF-DETERMINATION

WEDNESDAY, APRIL 8, 2015

U.S. SENATE,
COMMITTEE ON INDIAN AFFAIRS,
Crow Agency, MT.

The Committee met, pursuant to notice, at 10:30 a.m. in room 628, Little Big Horn College Health and Wellness Center, Crow Agency, Hon. Steve Daines, U.S. Senator from Montana, presiding.
[Opening prayer and drum ceremony performed.]
[Introductions by Robert Oldhorn.]

OPENING STATEMENT OF HON. STEVE DAINES, U.S. SENATOR FROM MONTANA

Senator DAINES. Thank you for that very warm introduction.

And I also want to thank all the Crow legislative and executive officials that are also here. We are very glad that they are here. I understand nearly all of them are here. It is a real honor that you have all made it.

We've got a lot to cover today, and so I call this hearing to order.

Today, the Committee will examine Empowering of Indian Country, Coal, Jobs, and Self-Determination.

It's an honor to be on the Crow Reservation here today examining an issue that means a great deal not only to Indian Country, but to all Montanans and Americans.

What gets lost in the debate back in Washington about energy development in general, and coal in particular, is what it means to real people in real places like Crow Agency, Montana, Where this is not some abstract policy, not some abstract debate in the halls of Congress, but this is a debate about the lives of real people. This is a debate about the future of sovereign nations looking to be self-sufficient and providing for their own livelihood.

The key issue for today's hearing, I believe, is jobs and the numbers are absolutely staggering.

According to the Montana Chamber of Commerce and Chairman Darrin Old Coyote, who we're going to hear from today, the unemployment rate on the Crow Reservation is 47 percent. But without the jobs provided by coal production, that number will climb to something greater than 80 percent.

I want to thank the Little Big Horn College for hosting us today, and particularly President David Yarlott. Your staff has been great to work with, and your facility is beautiful.

I can tell you this dais up here is so much more beautiful than we have back in Washington, D.C. So, truly, it is an honor to be here today, and your very, very warm welcome.

Additionally, Chairman Old Coyote, we appreciate the hospitality from the Crow Tribe, not just for this hearing but for the last several years.

I am also grateful to Attorney General Tim Fox for making the trip to be here—I know it was an early start for him to come down—and for his hard work defending Montana on energy policy and a whole host of other issues.

I also want to thank the Chairman of the Senate Committee on Indian Affairs. That's my colleague from Wyoming, Senator John Barrasso, along with the ranking member of the Committee, Senator John Tester, who couldn't make it to today's hearing.

It's an honor to work with them on these important issues on behalf of Indian County. And I'm glad the members of their staff could be here today, including the Committee staff directors, Mike and Tony. Thank you for making the trip here.

Well, today we're going to hear from witnesses who are experiencing the effects of bad policy in Washington that was developed from a top down approach, rather than listening to the folks with opinions that matter most, and that's those whose economic well-being depends on the coal industry to provide good paying jobs right here in Montana, right here in Indian Country.

Our young people shouldn't have to move far away just to make ends meet and raise a family, especially when the resources we need to power our schools, our homes, our factories across America are right here in our backyard. We must be responsible stewards of the land when we develop our resources, but we must also be responsible stewards of our children's futures.

So, while we'll hear from our witnesses about the devastating effects that the Obama Administration's clean power regulations would have upon the ability of Indian Tribes to sell their coal, we will also learn about specific opportunities to lift Tribal Nations out of poverty and take their rightful place as sovereign nations working with the Federal Government as a partner, not simply beholden to the whims of bureaucrats who live thousands of miles away.

The EPA was invited to testify at today's hearing, but they declined to do so, though, I am grateful that they have sent a representative from Helena, EPA State Director, Julie, here to listen to the comments from the hearing and from the audience.

I strongly encourage the EPA to listen closely to those most directly affected by their policies and request that today's message reaches Washington, D.C.

Additionally, export terminal projects, currently under review by the Corps of Engineers, have the potential to create several million dollars of tax revenue for local communities, and would ensure that states and Tribal Nations have access to new export opportunities in order to get a fair market value for their products.

The decision to approve port terminals especially in the Pacific Northwest, should take into consideration the effect on impacted Tribal Nations, and the states would benefit from access to international markets for products right here in the heart of Montana.

It is my understanding that the Corps of Engineers also has a representative here today, which I am thankful for, and I hope this hearing will bring to light important information considering approval for these export terminals.

In addition to insuring access to export markets for coal produced here in Montana, the Indian Coal Production Tax Credit, which expired at the end of 2014, after a one-year extension, must be made permanent.

For those who have spent time on the Crow Reservation, the economic benefits are self-evident. The Indian Coal Production Tax Credit has worked as a catalyst towards creating jobs and fostering tribal self-determination.

A study of preliminary findings was published in January of 2014 by the Harvard Project on American Indian Economic Development which demonstrated how essential this tax credit is to the economy of the Crow Reservation.

I look forward to learning more about the research findings during the course of this hearing today.

Well, we're a long ways away from Washington, D.C., and you know what, that's all right in my book.

I'll be taking the ideas that we will examine in today's hearing back to Congress so the voices of Montanans, the voices of the folks out here in Indian Country who are calling for a change in how business is done, that their voice will and can be heard.

So, today, we'll be hearing from a great panel. We'll be hearing from the Honorable Darrin Old Coyote, Chairman of the Crow Tribe of Montana, Crow Agency, Montana.

Chairman Old Coyote has become a good friend of mine in the past couple of years, and I enjoy working with him on issues that matter to the Crow people and all Montanans.

I know that the Chairman here is grateful about his people. And I'm proud to have a note from his daughter, Evelyn, who was just nine years old when she wrote it and presented it to me back in Washington. I have it displayed in my office today back in Washington. Evelyn is now 11.

You know what that note says? It says, ''Please keep the coal tax credit going——

[Applause.]

——to help me and other Crow kids have a brighter future.'' That is out of the mouth of a nine-year old.

Speaking as the father of four myself, I know that our kids' future motivates both me and the Chairman as we work together on coal and other issues that matter that we are facing here.

We also have with us today the Honorable Tim Fox, Attorney General of Montana and the Montana Department of Justice in Helena.

Attorney General Fox, I'm sure you're glad to be back in your home turf. He's a Hardin boy originally. We appreciate you made the long trip from Helena to be here today.

The Attorney General left about 4 o'clock this morning, no staff, and he drove down here by himself to be a part of this hearing, which we are grateful for.

Your work on the defending the rights of tribes and the development of coal has shown your commitment to this area that you call home.

Attorney General Fox has testified before Congress and the EPA's Clean Coal Regulation, and where lucky to have him as an advocate for Montana and for Indian Country.

His work on this is greatly appreciated, and I'm glad to have him as a teammate in promoting energy development, even though we root for different sides in the Cat/Griz games.

I have Grizzly bumper stickers on my pickup today because I lost a bet last fall. We're going to keep this as bipartisan as we can.

The Honorable Lorenzo Bates, Speaker of the Navajo Nation Council, Window Rock, Arizona has made this long trip. Welcome to Big Sky Country. We're very glad to have you here. It is an honor to have you here to show this isn't just a Montana issue, but one that affects tribes in places like Arizona as well.

Speaker Bates is a strong advocate for coal and energy development, and it's great to see another tribal leader who is aware of the importance of coal on their economic portfolio.

I know the Crow Tribe is glad to the Navajo as an ally in this fight. Thank you.

Jason Small is a journeyman boilermaker, labor advocate, a member of the Northern Cheyenne Tribe. Jason Small is a passionate advocate for resource development.

I had the pleasure of first meeting him for the first time at a Northern Cheyenne Council a couple years ago, where tribal leadership there over in Lame Deer told me I was the first Republican Congressman to ever meet with them at the tribal headquarters in Lame Deer.

Since that first meeting, Jason and I have become friends, and I had the pleasure of giving him a late night tour of the Capitol back in D.C. a while ago.

Jason returned the favor a few months later when he guided me through a boiler during spring overhaul at the power plant.

Jason is a great spokesperson for Montana coal, for the opportunities coal holds for Indian Country, and for the careers that coal provides to boilermakers, electrical workers, and other trades here in Montana.

And lastly, we have Eric Henson, research fellow, Harvard Project on American Indian Economic Development from Boston, Massachusetts.

As we'll hear in his testimony today, Eric Henson and his colleagues at Harvard University have done impressive research on how the economic situation of Tribal Nations, including the Crow Nation, and the importance that coal plays in their economic portfolio.

We are appreciative of him making the long journey to be here with us today. And also, as a member of the Chickasaw Nation, Mr. Henson brings a valuable academic perspective for discussion, and I look forward to your testimony.

I want to remind the witnesses that your full written testimony will be made part of the official hearing record. Please keep your statements to approximately five minutes so we may have time for questions.

I look forward to hearing your testimony, beginning with Chairman Old Coyote.

Please proceed.

STATEMENT OF HON. DARRIN OLD COYOTE, CHAIRMAN, CROW NATION

Mr. OLD COYOTE. Senator Daines, I want to thank you, Chairman Barrasso, Vice Chairman Tester, and members of the Committee for holding this Oversight Field Hearing on Coal, Jobs, and Self-Determination.

My name is Darrin Old Coyote. I am the Chairman of the Crow Nation.

The Crow Nation is honored to host this field hearing in Crow Country. We welcome all of our guests, including the Navajo Nation, other witnesses, Committee staff, federal agency representatives and the public to discuss this important subject.

I would also like to thank President Yarlott of Big Horn College for hosting us today.

As we develop our natural resources and diversified revenue, Little Big Horn College has, and will, continue to help to provide our tribaal citizens with education and training in numerous fields for new job opportunities.

Today, there are more than 13,000 enrolled citizens of the Crow Nation with approximately 9,000 of those residing on or near the reservation.

My administration's goal is to invite more of our citizens to return home to their relatives, but we must be able to offer homes, jobs and a place to realize their dreams.

Our employment rate remains too high. It's 47 percent.

The Crow Nation has 9 billion tons of recoverable coal with our longtime mining partner, Westmoreland.

The existing Absaloka Mine has supplied 180 million tons of Crow coal to Midwestern utilities since 1974. From the mine's annual production, the taxes and royalties to the Crow Nation represent as much as two-thirds of the Crow Nation's non-federal budget.

Also, the mine employs a 70 percent tribal workforce, with an average annual salary of over $66,000.

For two generations of the Crow leadership, we have simply sought to obtain full value for our coal resource. In fact, the last three administrations have testified in Congress that we repeatedly face obstacles in development despite consistent Crow leadership officials decisions to monetize their coal.

I, like my predecessors, simply want what is best for the Crow people.

We have a new barrier to Crow coal development. The EPA's Clean Power Plan Rule is a major problem for the Crow Nation.

The EPA did not consult with the Crow Nation, did not consider the economic impacts on the Crow Nation, and did not provide a less intrusive alternative to the severe effect on the Crow people.

In sum, the EPA violated its trust responsibility to the Crow Nation and must provide mitigation and transition time for the proposed Clean Power Plan Rule.

The proposed rule unfairly penalizes Midwest customers that currently buy and rely on production of Crow coal for its mix of energy production.

The local Minnesota utility and the powerplant have already publicly announced actions to comply with the EPA's plan and reduce carbon emissions.

The net effect will be a substantial loss of that market for Crow coal, thereby drastically reducing the Crow Nation's operating revenues and causing the loss of basic services and much needed employment on the Crow Reservation.

The Crow Nation has carefully examined its options for providing future economic opportunities for its members and has elected to monetize its coal asset by continuing to sell it for domestic power generation and exporting it to international markets.

The existing and future growth in the international energy markets for Crow coal provides an opportunity for the Crow Nation to obtain full value for our resource and would offset their loss of revenue caused by the EPA's decisions.

The Crow Nation has partnered with Cloud Peak Energy to develop the Big Metal Project and lease up to 1.4 billion tons of coal from the Crow Reservation's southeast corner.

In developing the Big Metal Mine project on Crow lands, the Crow Nation has a vital interest in a fact-based, timely decision on the Gateway Pacific Terminal project in Whatcom County, Washington state as an export terminal for Crow coal.

While not directly related to the development of the Big Metal Mine, a marine export facility is necessary infrastructure for supporting the full realization for the Crow Nation of the economic opportunity for our coal.

Crow recognizes attaining the full economic value for the Crow coal resource requires meeting existing and future international coal energy demand.

Therefore, Crow interests are aligned with the success of the Gateway Pacific Terminal and the connecting rail infrastructure.

Here at the Crow Indian Days and the Crow Nation Coal Summit in June, 2014, I invited Cloud Peak Energy, Burlington Northern Railway and SSA Marine to Crow Agency to see firsthand what coal means to Crow people.

At the summit, I observed the need for closer collaboration between the four partners, with each of us having a better chance of success by sharing information and working together on the export project.

This leadership was the start of a mutually supportive partnership between the four partners that exist today.

I would like to address the issue that has been raised by export opponents and addressed by Burlington Northern, coal dust.

In fact, coal dust was an issue that Burlington Northern first identified a decade ago as a contributer to derailments in mine holding areas. After studying the implementation steps to counter loads and apply vacuums in coal loading areas, coal dust was largely eliminated.

Burlington Northern Santa Fe has been hauling coal for export through the Pacific Northwest for decades, and during that time has not received any complaints from a natural resource agency about coal dust until after the Gateway Pacific Terminal was announced.

To aggressively address opponents' foundation for lingering concerns about coal dust, Burlington Northern Santa Fe took the added step to salvage a second vacuum spray facility in Pasco, Washington at the east end of the Columbia River Gorge.

BNSF has also sought an independent third-party system of coal dust. The U.S. Department of Transportation, National Transportation System Center is currently engaged in a full coal dust research study.

All of these steps represent a comprehensive commitment by BNSF to eliminate any various allegations about coal dust.

The Crow Nation recognizes the national importance of the Gateway Pacific Terminal as the best potential new site to ship U.S. cargos through U.S. ports.

Along with partnering with Cloud Peak and BNSF Railway, the Crow Nation has partnered with Washington state-based terminal developer, SSA Marine.

SSA Marine has secured 1,500 acres of private property, and the heavy impact industrial zone at Cherry Point in Washington State. In February, 2011, they submitted applications to develop and operate the proposed Gateway Pacific Terminal bulk quantity marine shipping facility.

The terminal is designed to process up to 48 million tons of coal, and would be the fourth pier at Cherry Point, located next to three existing refineries.

There are existing heavy industrial utilities and existing rail line on the property. Even more important is the naturally occurring deep water requiring no dredging to construct a wharf that will accommodate deep-draft Capesize bulk cargo vessels.

Approximately 75 percent of the cost of landing U.S. bulk cargo in Asia is related to transportation.

Shipping U.S. commodities in Capesize vessels can cut overall ocean transportation costs by 20 to 30 percent. This is an important factor allowing Crow and other U.S. producers to be competitive in the growing Asian market.

The terminal is being designed and engineered to meet Washington state's high environmental standards and is already undergoing a rigorous evaluation in an EIS.

The State Environmental Policy Act EIS review is led by Whatcom County and the Washington Department of Ecology. The U.S. Army Corps of Engineers is the federal lead agency for the National Environmental Policy Act EIS.

The State and Federal EIS will provide the basis for making informed decisions on the terminal project.

Similar to the big metal mine provided for the economic future of the Crow Nation, the privately funded Gateway Pacific Terminal Project will provide a lift to the local economy during construction and a permanent boost in Whatcom County's industrial sector with hundreds of new, permanent family-waged jobs.

That is why the Gateway Pacific Terminal Project enjoys broad support from the national AFL–CIO, Montana State AFL–CIO, Northwest Washington Central Legal Council, to name just a few, construction will generate approximately 4,430 direct and indirect jobs and nearly $92 million in state and local taxes over two years.

When operating at full capacity, the terminal will sustain approximately 1250 permanent direct and indirect jobs and generate about $11 million annually in local and state tax revenues.

Investments in export terminals, particularly the Gateway Pacific Terminal will improve critical infrastructure and create economic wealth to both the Pacific Northwest and for the Crow Nation.

Today, the Crow Nation desires to develop its vast coal resources not only for itself, but for our energy partners, the surrounding communities and for the United States.

By developing Crow coal via domestic markets, export terminals and coal conversion, we firmly believe that we can help ourselves while simultaneously meeting national energy goals, achieving energy independence, securing a domestic supply of valuable energy, and, reducing the country's dependence on foreign oil.

My administration has been very busy in working to develop our coal resources and to remove obstacles to successful development.

I simply desire for the Crow Nation to become self-sufficient by developing our own coal resources and to provide basic services for the health, hopes and future of the Crow people.

It is also important to understand that this is our permanent homeland, and we will always take care of it as responsible developers.

With help from you, our historic treaty ally, in leveling the energy development playing field, we can achieve my vision and both benefit immensely.

Senator Daines, thank you again for the opportunity to testify on this critical subject before you today. Thank you.

[The prepared statement of Mr. Old Coyote follows:]

PREPARED STATEMENT OF HON. DARRIN OLD COYOTE, CHAIRMAN, CROW NATION

I. Introduction

Good morning. On behalf of the Crow Nation, I want to thank Chairman Barrasso, Vice-Chairman Tester, Senator Daines and the members of the Senate Committee on Indian Affairs for holding this Oversight Field Hearing on Empowering Indian Country. My name is Darrin Old Coyote and I am the Chairman of the Crow Nation. I appreciate this invitation to provide testimony from the Crow Nation's perspective on coal development, an area central to my administration and a topic that has unlimited potential to improve the ongoing substandard socioeconomic conditions of the Crow people and the surrounding communities in southeastern Montana (the northern portion of the Powder River Basin) and northern Wyoming.

I have served as an elected official of the Crow Nation for over 10 years. Over the past 2 years, with the help of our coal partners and the Crow Nation Legislative Branch, we have taken several meaningful steps toward the successful development of our coal resources and look forward to completing, in the next few years, projects that will positively transform my community. My purpose today is to provide a brief history of the Crow Nation's resources, to summarize my administration's efforts to develop Crow coal in the northern Powder River Basin, and to share the benefits and challenges of Crow coal development.

II. Brief Overview of Crow Reservation, Land Issues and Resources

A. Brief History of Land and Development Challenges

The Crow Nation is a sovereign government located in southeastern Montana. The Crow Nation has three formal treaties with the Federal Government, concluding with the Fort Laramie Treaty of May 7, 1868. The Crow Reservation originally encompassed most of Wyoming (including the Powder River Basin) and southeastern Montana, totaling 38.5 million acres. Through a series of treaties, agreements and unilateral federal laws over a 70 year span, Crow territory was reduced by 94 percent to its current 2.2 million acre area.

In addition to substantial land loss, the remaining tribal land base within the exterior boundary of the Crow Reservation was carved up by the 1920 Crow Allotment Act. In 1919, prior to the Allotment Act, there were 2,453 allotments (individual Crow ownership), consisting of 482,584 acres. By 1935, there were 5,507 Crow allotments, consisting of 2,054,055 acres (218,136 acres were alienated by 1935). The Big Horn and Pryor Mountains were not allotted and still remain reserved for the Crow Nation and its citizens.

Because of allotment and federal probate of Indian property (with many Indians dying without wills), the phenomenon of fractionated land ownership arose—where several (sometimes hundreds of) owners might have varying interests in a single parcel. By 1928, the Meriam Report declared the federal allotment policy to be one of the most disastrous federal policies of all time. During discussions leading up to the *Indian Reorganization Act* of 1934, one congressman explained the fractionating effects of allotment in this fashion:

> "It is in the case of the inherited allotments, however, that the administrative costs become incredible. . . . On allotted reservations, numerous cases exist where the shares of each individual heir from lease money may be 1 cent a month. Or one heir may own minute fractional shares in 30 or 40 different allotments. The cost of leasing, bookkeeping, and distributing the proceeds in many cases far exceeds the total income. The Indians and the Indian Service personnel are thus trapped in a meaningless system of minute partition in which all thought of the possible use of land to satisfy human needs is lost in a mathematical haze of bookkeeping." 78 Cong.Rec. 11728 (1934), cited in *Hodel v. Irving*, 481 U.S. 704 (U.S.S.D. 1987).

The Crow land base had been decimated by fractionated ownership of various allotments. The Department of the Interior (DOI) estimated that over 10 percent of all fractionated lands within Indian country are actually within the Crow Reservation (with numerous parcels of allotted lands that have more than 10 owners and sometimes more than 100 owners).

Recently, the Crow Nation partnered with DOI and meaningfully addressed the fractionation issue through implementation of the *Cobell* Settlement. As of March 2016, the Crow Land Buy-Back Program (LBBP) had a willing buyer—willing purchaser success rate of 64 percent (Crow allottees sold their interests in various parcels of land to DOI in trust for the Crow Nation). The Crow LBBP resulted in more than $130 million paid out to Crow landowners, with more than 240,000 equivalent acres purchased for the Crow Nation. The original intent of reducing fractionation was accomplished and, simultaneously, the Crow Nation can make more of the Crow homeland productive for both residential and energy development purposes.

However, the overall loss of the Crow land base and allotment have collectively resulted in checkerboard ownership of reservation lands, giving rise to overlapping governmental authority in Indian country (federal, state, tribal and local). Sometimes, the land issues become cost prohibitive for some project developers. As discussed later, tax incentives are critical in order to level the playing field for Indian energy projects.

B. Present Land, Population, and Education

The statistical land ownership resulting from the above described legal history (and successful fraction reduction efforts) is approximately: 32 percent Crow allotments; 33 percent Crow Nation trust and fee land; and 35 percent non-Indian fee land (basically 2/3 of surface land is owned by the Crow Nation and individual Crows). However, overall, the pattern of surface ownership generally is "checkerboard" with interspersed Crow Nation trust and fee lands, Crow allotments and non-Indian fee lands. At times, the checkerboard nature of the surface ownership creates challenges, summarized later, for developing the subsurface minerals (almost all of which is owned by the Crow Nation).

Today, there are more than 13,000 enrolled citizens of the Crow Nation, with approximately 9,000 of those residing within the exterior boundaries of the Reservation. Our goal is to invite more of our citizens to return home to live and resume tribal relations, but we must be able to offer homes, jobs, and a place to find their dreams. Our current unemployment rate is 47 percent. The Crow Nation has always emphasized higher education and we currently have more than 400 annual applications for higher education assistance. Because of federal funding limitations and internal budget constraints, however, we can only partially fund 90 students each year.

In addition to providing financial support for education, we have a separately chartered tribal college (Little Bighorn College, ''LBHC'') that started operations in 1981. Among the hundreds of LBHC graduates, many are employed on and around the Crow Reservation in a variety of positions including teachers' aides, computer technicians, office managers and administrative assistants. At least sixty have completed bachelor's degrees and are pursuing professions in education, social work, human services, science, nursing, technology, accounting and business. As we move forward in developing our coal resources, LBHC can help to provide our citizens with training in fields for new job opportunities.

C. Coal—Past and Present

The Crow Nation has very substantial undeveloped coal resources. In fact, today, the Crow Indian Reservation contains 2 million acres in subsurface mineral rights, including an estimated 9 billion tons of coal. The Crow Nation has developed a limited amount of its resource, by leasing a portion of its coal reserves for 40 continuous years to Westmoreland Resources, Inc. (WRI). WRI owns and operates the Absaloka Mine (''Mine''), a 15,000-acre single pit surface coal mine complex near Hardin, Montana, on the northern border of the Crow Reservation.

The Absaloka Mine was developed to supply Powder River Basin coal to Midwestern utilities and it has produced over 180 million tons of coal since 1974. From the Mine's 5–7 million tons per year of coal production, it provides production taxes and royalties to the Crow Nation—exceeding $20 million in 2010 when the Mine was operating at full capacity. The revenue generated from the Mine represents as much as two-thirds of the Crow Nation's non-federal budget.

Furthermore, WRI employs a 70 percent tribal workforce, with an average annual salary of over $66,000, and a total employment expense of approximately $18.6 million dollars. The Absaloka Mine is the largest private employer within the Crow Reservation. The importance of the Mine to the economy of the Crow Reservation cannot be overstated. Without question, it is a critical source of jobs, financial support and domestically-produced energy. WRI has been the Crow Nation's most significant private partner over the past 40 years.

A recent example demonstrates the importance of the Absaloka Mine to the Crow people. A major unplanned outage at the Mine's largest power plant customer during 2011–2013 resulted in a 50 percent reduction in tribal coal revenue and numerous employment layoffs. This recent outage reinforced the need for the Crow Nation to pursue multiple coal projects to diversify our revenue base.

III. My Administration's Vision on Energy Development: Potential Benefits

Given our vast mineral resources, the Crow Nation can, and should, be self-sufficient. My goal is clear. My administration desires to develop our mineral resources in an economically sound, environmentally responsible manner that is consistent with Crow culture and beliefs. More than anything, I desire to improve the Crow people's quality of life, create a future with good-paying jobs and employment benefits within the Crow Reservation, and provide hope and prosperity for the next seven generations of Crow citizens.

My larger vision is to become America's energy partner and help reduce America's dependence on foreign oil. Over the next 40 years, the World Energy Council predicts that the world will need to double today's level of energy supply to meet increased demand. Primary energy sources, such as coal, oil and gas, have a finite life and therefore we must have an all-of-the-above energy development strategy to meet America's needs as well as global demand.

My administration stands ready to meet the global energy challenge, but the future both near and long term, must have coal in its equation. With President Obama's recent speech on climate change, we are mindful of the increased efforts, policy and otherwise, to restrict coal as a domestic fossil fuel source to generate electricity (with domestic coal produced electricity being reduced from approximately 50 percent to 40 percent in less than a decade). Our coal partners and our coal economist consistently remind us of the difficult environment for domestic coal production.

Despite the challenging environment, the Crow Nation has intensified its efforts to develop its coal resources to diversify its revenue streams. With respect to the Absaloka Mine, the Crow Tribal Legislature approved and I executed an agreement with WRI in March 2013 to expand its mining operations with a lease of an estimated 145 million tons of Rosebud-McKay seam coal resources located adjacent to the Mine. This new lease will provide the Crow Nation with long-term revenues and employment and sustain the operations of the Mine past 2020.

Similarly, in June 2013, the BIA approved another tribally-approved agreement with Cloud Peak Energy (CPE) to explore, with options to lease and develop an estimated 1.4 billion tons of Crow coal in the southeastern corner of the Crow Reservation. This long-term agreement will also provide much needed revenue to the Crow Nation, increase employment opportunities for Crow and Montana citizens, and diversify Tribal revenue sources. However, the CPE project—named Big Metal (*www.bigmetalcoal.com*), is largely dependent on coal exports through the Northwest.

As such, I have directed my administration to investigate and pursue coal exports, given the increased coal demand in the Pacific Rim. Since 2013, I have sent three Crow delegations to the Northwest to meet and work with other tribal nations, investigate proposed coal export projects, and then to analyze and follow-up on these recent diplomatic discussions and fact-finding trips about possible relationships involving Crow coal, transportation, and export terminal partners. During the last two trips, which I attended, I invited present and potential project partners, as well as tribal leaders from Northwest tribal nations, to visit my homeland to see first-hand Crow coal development and listen to their concerns.

The last two summers I have hosted a Crow Nation Coal Summit to answer questions about coal transportation issues (coal dust and train traffic), jobs (viewing Crow citizens at the Absaloka Mine), reclamation and the potential for future export development. We worked with our coal partners to provide mine tours of CPE's Spring Creek and WRI's Absaloka mine, to provide coal transportation information from BNSF Railway (BNSF) representatives, and to have coal export terminal questions answered by representatives from SSA Marine, the project developers of the proposed Gateway Pacific Terminal marine export facility.

We have been made aware of local concerns regarding coal export projects expressed by citizens in the Northwest. That is the reason I brought industry, tribal nations and local citizens together to inform, educate, and work with each other to address any substantive issues. I will continue to work with everyone and respect tribal treaty rights and local concerns. However, I strongly feel that non-governmental organizations cannot and should not tell me to leave Crow coal in the ground; I was elected to provide basic services and jobs to my citizens and I will steadfastly and responsibly pursue Crow coal development to achieve my vision for the Crow people.

Finally, with a substantial Crow coal resource, I would like to continue to build the first coal-to-liquids (CTL) plant in North America with carbon capture and utilization. In fact, in 2008, the Crow Nation and our partner signed a project agreement to develop Many Stars, a planned coal-to-liquids project that sought to produce up to 50,000 barrels or more per day of ultra-clean jet and diesel fuel. Crow sought to contract with the U.S. Air Force and other local industries to supply clean diesel fuel that would meaningfully reduce carbon emissions throughout the world, reduce America's dependence on foreign oil, and provide a safe and secure domestic fuel supply to our national defense.

Unfortunately, the economic recession hit and an uncertain national energy policy made it difficult for the proposed project to proceed. We remain hopeful that the Administration can and will support clean coal, that technology advancements can create a smaller scale project, and that clean coal legislation (discussion draft entitled, "Native American Clean Coal Economic Development Act of 2015") to provide for bonding authority with incentives to industry partners will be introduced and passed in this Congress. I am pursuing an all-of-the-above energy development strategy (hydropower, wind, coal export and CTL) but I will need some help in order to effectuate my energy vision.

IV. Challenges and the Need to Level the Playing Field

A. EPA's Clean Power Plan

The Crow Nation and the Montana Attorney General sent joint comments to the EPA on December 1, 2014, to express grave concern about the substantial negative impact that the EPA's Proposed Rule, dated June 18, 2014, and titled, "Carbon Pollution Emission Guidelines for Existing Stationary Sources: Electric Utility Generating Units," will have on the Crow Nation, its citizens and resources, and their collective future. In sum, both the Proposed Rule dated June 18, 2014, and the subsequent and separate proposed Clean Power Plan Rule for Indian country dated November 4, 2014, simply ignore the Crow Nation's concerns.

The lack of meaningful government-to-government consultation, as required by Executive Order 13175, in developing the aforementioned Proposed Rules is telling. Despite minimal tribal outreach (and no direct contact with elected Crow Nation officials before the rule was proposed), significant substantive policy prescriptions are likely to cause serious setbacks to the Crow Nation, potentially over multiple generations. The longstanding trust responsibility between the Federal Government and the Crow Nation may be violated unless an exception and/or mitigation of the rule is provided to us.

The Proposed Rule is a major problem for the Crow Nation. The EPA did not consult with the Crow Nation, did not consider the economic impacts on the Crow Nation, and did not provide a less intrusive alternative to the severe effect on the Crow Nation of this Proposed Rule. In sum, the EPA violated its trust responsibility to the Crow Nation and must provide a substantive alternative and/or mitigation of the Proposed Rule.

i. The agency failed in its duties to consult with the Crow Nation and to consider the economic effects of the proposal on the Crow Nation.

As mentioned above, the Crow Nation receives revenues equaling 66 percent of its annual non-federal budget from severance taxes and royalties paid for the mining of coal owned by the Crow Nation at the Mine, near Hardin, Montana. Ninety percent of the coal mined from the Mine is sold to, and burned at, electrical generating units (EGU) in Minnesota. The Proposed Rule strongly encouraged the State of Minnesota to demand retirement of the older units of the power plant to meet the carbon reduction goals set by the EPA.

The Proposed Rule also sets higher renewable standards for the State of Minnesota to meet by 2030, despite Minnesota law already requiring higher levels of renewable energy to be produced by 2020. Because the Proposed Rule will unfairly penalize Minnesota and other Midwest customers that currently buy and rely on production of Crow coal for its mix of energy production, and since the Minnesota EGU have already taken action to reduce carbon emissions, the result will be a substantial loss of that market for Crow coal.

That in turn will mean drastic hits to the Crow Nation's operating revenues, which will directly cause the loss of services and employment on the Crow Reservation. Despite Executive Orders requiring federal agencies to engage in substantive consultation with Indian Tribes affected by agency proposals, and to consider the impact of proposals on economic growth and job creation, the EPA utterly failed to do so with respect to the effect of this proposal on the Crow Nation.

Executive Order 13175 requires agencies to ensure meaningful and timely input by tribal officials in the development of regulatory policies that affect tribes. In this case, that simply didn't happen. Despite representations at Section III.A.5 of the Proposed Rules that the ''EPA conducted significant outreach to tribes,'' the actual extent of the agency's effort was minimal, at best. Other than a letter purportedly sent to the Tribe (a form letter stating, ''Dear Tribal Leader''), no one in the agency contacted the Crow Nation directly—government-to-government—as is required in the aforementioned Executive Order and Presidential Memo that implements EO 13175.

The lack of meaningful consultation is perplexing in light of the fact that the Crow Nation is one of only four tribes nationwide that owns merchantable coal deposits, and is one of only three tribes (out of 566 federally recognized tribes) for whom the mining of coal burned in electrical generating units impacted by the proposal is a hugely significant piece of the Tribal economy. Because the Crow Nation only produces coal with its longstanding development partner and there is not a coal-fired power plant on the Crow Reservation, the EPA Proposed Clean Power Plan for Indian country (those tribes with EGUs within their reservation boundaries) also does not apply.

The November 4, 2014, Clean Power Plan Rule simply provides an option for a tribe to develop its own Section 111(d) plan and, if they choose not to, then the EPA would develop a federal plan necessary to achieve the EPA's suggested carbon emission reductions in Indian country. Since the Crow Nation does not have an EGU on its reservation, the Clean Power Plan Rule is inapplicable to the Crow Nation. Therefore, both sets of the EPA's Proposed Rules do not address the Crow Nation's significant interests impacted as a result of federal agency action.

Furthermore, Executive Order 13563 requires federal agencies to propose or adopt a regulation only upon a reasoned determination that its benefits justify its costs and to tailor its regulations to impose the least burden on society consistent with regulatory objectives. It requires that regulations be based on an open exchange of information and perspectives among State, local and Tribal officials. Any open exchange with Crow Tribal officials would have brought to light the impact of the proposal on the Crow Nation and would have highlighted the unfairly prejudicial impact of the proposal on the Minnesota customer of Crow coal.

B. Practical Challenges

In addition to the EPA's Clean Power Plan, numerous practical problems consistently arise with each proposed Indian coal project. The lease approval and development process is burdensome, slow, and complicated. Federal regulatory requirements for appraisals, surface access approvals and environmental assessments to conduct exploration within the Reservation often create significant delays. Further, incomplete land records (in some cases BIA records for surface and mineral ownership are erroneous, missing and out of date), inadequate BIA staffing (e.g., the BIA area office in Billings, Montana, has one primary individual to work on environmental issues for eight tribal nations), and surface land fractionation (described above) create uncertainty that discourages investment and significantly impedes project development.

It is extremely difficult to compete with off-reservation development because of these problems. Many companies view these additional regulatory and practical burdens as cost prohibitive, even with the best efforts of particular BIA employees and the Crow Nation. Based on our experience in working with current and prospective coal partners, we strongly recommend a two-prong approach to leveling the playing field for energy development in Crow country: (i) eliminate regulatory obstacles (we provided written support for H.R. 1548, Native American Energy Act); and (ii) permanently extend existing tax incentives to offset the extra development burdens.

C. Leveling the Playing Field

There are a few federal tax incentives that encourage investment and development in Indian country, but their utility is diminished by their short-term nature. Accelerated depreciation and the Indian employment tax credit are two examples of such incentives (the latter needs some modifications to enhance its effectiveness). These incentives, originally enacted in the 1993 Budget Reconciliation Act, have been extended year-to-year in the tax extenders package and, as such, generally are not relied upon by potential investors with large Indian energy projects because of the extended length of time (often 5–10 years for large coal projects) that development takes before the energy commodity is produced. The Crow Nation supports the permanent extension of these tax incentives, with modifications, but another more specific tax incentive is the most important for Crow coal development.

The Indian coal production tax credit (ICPTC), originally enacted in the 2005 Energy Policy Act, has kept the Absaloka Mine open and competitive since 2006. This credit neutralized the threat of a potential mine closure and also continued WRI's ability to provide critical employment and revenue for essential Crow governmental functions. Like the aforementioned tax incentives, it expired on December 31, 2014, and continues to be part of the overall tax extenders package.

In order to overcome all of the additional regulatory costs and land transaction issues described above, the Crow Nation seeks a permanent extension of ICPTC, with a few modifications. We would like for the ICPTC to be used against the alternative minimum tax, to extend the placed in service date to include the aforementioned projects, and to eliminate the unrelated person requirement in the original credit (to allow for a CTL project in the future). With these tax incentives made permanent, the Crow Nation would have the opportunity to compete with others on a level playing field.

V. Market Access for Crow Coal

A. Crow Tribe Interest in Infrastructure

The Crow Nation has carefully examined its options for providing future economic opportunity for its members and has elected to monetize its coal asset by continuing to selling it for domestic power generation and exporting it to international markets. The existing and future growth in the international energy markets for coal provides the opportunity for the Crow Nation to obtain full value for their resource and would offset their loss of revenue caused by the EPA's decisions.

In pursuit of exporting Crow coal, the Crow Nation is engaging in interstate commerce and international trade. Crow Nation has partnered with CPE, BNSF and SSA Marine to gain access to international markets and compete with other nations in supplying a secure source of energy to meet global demand to United States trading partners.

Powder River Basin coal is exported out of Canadian ports in British Columbia today. In the absence of U.S. port capacity, British Columbia ports have been expanding to receive U.S. cargoes. The Crow Nation recognizes the national importance of the Gateway Pacific Terminal as the best potential new site to ship U.S. cargoes through U.S. ports.

B. The Big Metal Mine Project

The Crow Nation is partnered with CPE on the Big Metal Project. The agreement is for the exploration and the option to lease up to 1.4 billion tons of coal from the Crow Reservation's southeast corner. CPE has demonstrated their commitment to both safety and the environment, and we appreciate their leadership as one of this country's largest coal producers. In addition, CPE has been a good partner with the Crow Nation, providing college scholarships to more than 40 Crow students and supporting those in need. All of this has happened while CPE has worked with the Tribe to complete exploratory drilling, which has been ongoing since June of 2014.

In developing the Big Metal Mine project on Crow lands, the Crow Nation has a vital interest in a fact-based, timely decision on the Gateway Pacific Terminal project in Whatcom County, Washington as an export terminal for Crow coal. While not directly related to the development of the Big Metal Mine, a marine export facility is necessary infrastructure for supporting the full realization for the Crow Nation of the economic opportunity for its coal. Crow recognizes attaining full economic value for the Crow coal resource requires meeting existing and future international coal energy demand; to that end, Crow interests are aligned with Gateway Pacific Terminal's success and the connecting rail infrastructure.

C. Energy Poverty and the Global and Asian-Pacific Coal Demand

Let me address a few key issues pertaining to coal and its place in the world's energy portfolio and in the amelioration of energy poverty. According to the International Energy Agency, 1.3 billion people are without access to electricity. That is 18-percent of the world's population or nearly 1 in 5 people. For many of these people, coal-fueled, low-cost, reliable electricity represents an opportunity to climb out of the misery of poverty.

Coal is an important component of the world's energy portfolio until better solutions are arrived at, especially in those countries that are in need of electrification to resolve poverty. A key goal of the Copenhagen Accord of 2010 is to provide energy to these impoverished populations. For the time being, coal is simply an essential source of fuel.

According to the International Energy Agency, global demand for coal will increase to more than 9 billion tons of coal by 2019 with much of that growth fueled by demand from Asia and India. Since the beginning of the 21st century, coal has been the fastest-growing global energy source worldwide. According to the U.S.'s Energy Information Administration, "Japan imported nearly 211 million short tons of coal in 2013, up from 204 million short tons in 2012, after more coal capacity came online." In addition, the Japanese are funding coal-fueled power plants in Japan and throughout Asia, leading to increased demand.

Bill Gates, himself a climate change activist, offered this observation on the present need for the use of fossil fuels in developing countries: "[People in poor countries] desperately need cheap sources of energy now to fuel the economic growth that lifts families out of poverty. They can't afford today's expensive clean energy solutions, and we can't expect them to wait for the technology to get cheaper." *Gatesnotes, The Blog of Bill Gates, June 25, 2014*

Independent experts at places like Stanford University state that U.S. coal exports will not increase the usage of coal in Asia, but will likely replace inferior sources of coal from other countries. As well, they have concluded that exporting U.S. coal will not increase greenhouse gas emissions and may actually reduce them.

As long as coal is to be utilized, from an environmental perspective, Powder River Basin coal is a preferred alternative (and has been called "clean coal" by the USGS), because it is lower in sulfur, ash, and other contaminants. As well, it is mined under the world's highest labor and environmental standards.

Cloud Peak Energy is the largest U.S. supplier of coal for electricity to South Korea. Last year alone, Cloud Peak Energy shipped 4 million tons to Asian utilities, many of whom are constructing the world's most-advanced coal-fueled power plants. According to the U.S. Energy Information Administration, "[c]oal consumption in South Korea increased by 55 percent between 2005 and 2012, driven primarily by growing demand from the electric power sector." South Korean utilities are currently adding even more coal-fueled power plants to meet the country's increasing need for electricity.

The increasing demand for power from coal has raised questions about air quality impacts, both locally and globally. It is important to note that Powder River Basin coal from Crow mines is lower in sulfur dioxide and nitrogen oxide, which is better for the environment than the coal that is currently mined in Asian countries. Together with modern power plant technology being developed in Asia, use of Powder River Basin coal may reduce, and not raise, global emissions of air pollutants and carbon emissions.

D. Rail Transportation

BNSF is the leading railroad in the U.S. with a network of 32,500 route miles, 48,000 employees and 8,000 locomotives. Montana and Wyoming are home to over 4,000 BNSF employees and their families. Payroll for these two states exceeds $300 million. BNSF is aggressively investing to preserve, maintain, and grow capacity across its 28-state network with a capital investment plan of over $5 billion in 2014 and $6 billion in 2015. Much of this investment is dedicated along its major coal routes.

BNSF Railway serves the Powder River Basin (PRB) region, transporting coal to customers throughout the Midwest and southern regions of the U.S., as well as to the west coast for export. Since 2000, BNSF has doubled coal delivery to Eastern customers from 50 to 100 million tons. In addition, BNSF delivers more coal than any other U.S. company, including 57 percent from the PRB region.

The Federal Railroad Administration determined that 2013 and 2014 were the safest in U.S. history for freight railroads. With major investment in infrastructure, safe operating practices, and a comprehensive safety culture, BNSF continues to make great strides in their highest priority of safety.

E. Gateway Pacific Terminal

The Terminal developer, SSA Marine, is a Washington State corporation founded in 1949 in Bellingham, Washington. They have grown to be the largest privately held terminal operating company in the world. In 1991, SSA Marine's subsidiary, Pacific International Terminals, Inc., secured the property at Cherry Point, Washington State. Since then, they have taken thoughtful steps to develop the 1,500-acre property located in Whatcom County, 17 miles south of the U.S.-Canadian border. Pacific International Terminals has committed to develop the Terminal while ensuring that the environment, the community and shippers' interests all benefit.

Pacific International Terminals submitted an application for project permits in February 2011 to develop and operate the proposed Gateway Pacific Terminal ("Terminal") as a multi-commodity bulk terminal for transshipment of dry bulk commodities between rail and marine transportation systems. It is intended to meet the need for a West Coast marine shipping facility to serve the transpacific market.

The Terminal is designed to process up to 54 million tons of dry bulk commodities annually, including up to 48 million tons of coal. Other potential cargoes are grains, potash and wood bio-fuels. It will be the fourth pier at Cherry Point, a designated Heavy Impact Industrial zone, located next to the existing BP Cherry Point Refinery, the ALCOA—Intalco Works aluminum smelter and Phillips 66 Ferndale Refinery.

Cherry Point is an ideal location for the Terminal. The existing heavy industrial utilities and existing rail line are essential for efficient operation of the marine shipping facility. Even more important is the naturally occurring deep water requiring no dredging to construct a wharf that will accommodate deep-draft "Capesize" bulk cargo vessels. The Terminal is adjacent to a designated international shipping corridor that is highly regulated by a Vessel Traffic System jointly operated by the U.S. and Canadian Coast Guards for over 40 years with great success.

The economies of scale of Capesize vessels allows them to be more fuel, carbon, and cost-efficient than smaller ships in moving a ton of product. Approximately 75 percent of the cost of landing U.S. bulk cargo in Asia is related to transportation. Shipping U.S. commodities in Capesize vessels can cut overall ocean transportation costs by 20–30 percent. This is an important factor allowing Crow and other U.S. producers to be competitive in the growing Asian markets.

The Terminal is being designed and engineered to meet Washington State's high environmental standards and is already undergoing a rigorous evaluation of the environmental, social, and economic benefits and impacts in an Environmental Impact Statement (EIS). The State Environmental Policy Act (SEPA) EIS, led by Whatcom County and the Washington Department of Ecology. The U.S. Army Corps of Engineers is the Federal lead agency for the National Environmental Policy Act (NEPA). The State and Federal EIS's will provide the basis for making informed decisions on the Terminal project.

The privately funded Terminal will provide a big lift to the local economy during construction, and a permanent boost in Whatcom County's industrial sector with hundreds of new, permanent family-wage jobs. Construction will generate approximately 4,430 direct and indirect jobs and nearly $92 million in state and local taxes over two years. When operating at full capacity, the Terminal will sustain approximately 1,250 permanent direct and indirect jobs and generate about $11 million annually in local and state tax revenues. Altogether, with the tax revenue and wages during two years of construction plus 10 years of full operations, the Terminal would bring more than $1.8 billion in revenue to the region.

VI. Conclusion

Today, the Crow Nation desires to develop its vast coal resources not only for itself, but for our energy partners, the surrounding communities and for the United States. By developing Crow coal via domestic markets, export terminals and coal conversion, we firmly believe we can help ourselves while simultaneously meeting national energy goals—achieving energy independence, securing a domestic supply of valuable energy, and reducing the country's dependence on foreign oil. My administration has been very busy in working to develop our coal resources and to remove obstacles to successful development.

I simply desire for the Crow Nation to become self-sufficient by developing its own coal resources and to provide basic services for the health, hopes and future of the Crow people. With help from you—our historic treaty ally—in leveling the energy development playing field, we can achieve my vision and both benefit immensely.

Mr. Chairman and Committee members, thank you again for the opportunity to testify on this critical subject before you today. I would be happy to answer any questions.

Addendum—Additional Crow Nation Perspective on World Energy Demand and Coal Exports

The Crow Nation has carefully examined its options for providing economic opportunity for its members and has elected to monetize its coal asset for export to Pacific Rim countries.

Global climate issues are an administration priority and the Crow people share the President's concern. Coal is an important component of the world's energy portfolio until better solutions are arrived at, especially in those countries that are in need of electrification to resolve poverty.[1][2] A key goal of the Copenhagen Accord of 2010 is to provide energy to these impoverished populations. For the time being, coal is simply an essential source of fuel.[3]

Bill Gates offered this observation on the present need for the use of fossil fuels in developing countries: ''[People in poor countries] desperately need cheap sources of energy now to fuel the economic growth that lifts families out of poverty. They can't afford today's expensive clean energy solutions, and we can't expect them wait for the technology to get cheaper.'' *Gatesnotes*, The Blog of Bill Gates, June 25, 2014

U.S. coal exports will not increase the usage of coal in Asia[4], but will likely replace inferior sources of coal from other countries. As long as coal is to be utilized, from an environmental perspective, Powder River Basin coal is a preferred alternative (and has been called ''clean coal'' by the USGS), because it is lower in sulfur, ash, and other contaminants.[5][9] As well, it is mined under the world's highest labor and environmental standards.

Exporting U.S. coal will not increase greenhouse gas emissions and may actually reduce them.[6] If the U.S. does not build the port capacity to export its own coal, then Canada and/or Mexico are likely to do so.[7]

The Crow need the option of shipping their product through an efficient west coast port. The proposed Gateway Pacific Terminal in northwest Washington would have a maximum coal exporting capacity of 48 million metric tons per year. (The facility is being proposed by Washington-based SSA Marine, which is the nation's leading shipping terminal operator with 125 locations worldwide.) Although this would be an economically transformative activity for the Crow people, it would constitute a tiny fraction of coal consumption in Asia.[8]

Crow coal exports will support the purposes of the administration's National Export Initiative and NEI/NEXT, and help to increase trade with other countries. As well, it is consistent with national policies (such as those articulated in the National Defense Authorization Act) that aim to support our Asian allies, who need affordable and geo-politically stable sources of fuel.

Freedom of interstate commerce and reservation of power to regulate commerce (national and tribal nations) to the Congress (as opposed to individual states) are foundational principles embedded in Article I, Section 3 of the U.S. Constitution. That same section reserves to the Congress the exclusive power to regulate commerce ''with the Indian tribes.'' The governments of North Dakota, Wyoming, and Montana have expressed concerns that the environmental review processes for west coast coal export projects are being used to interfere with constitutionally protected interstate commerce.

The export of Crow coal supports the people of the Crow Nation and is consistent with the federal government's constitutional and treaty trust obligations to the tribe.

Footnote References—*World Energy Demand and Coal Exports*

[1] The Global Energy Network Institute has confirmed, "Every single one of the United Nations' Millennium Development Goals requires access to electricity as a necessary prerequisite." The International Energy Agency's (IEA) Faith Birol, agrees and states, "The importance of coal in the global energy mix is now the highest since 1971. It remains the backbone of electricity generation and has been the fuel underpinning the rapid industrialization of emerging economies, helping to raise living standards and lift hundreds of millions of people out of poverty."
Letter from National Mining Association to Export-Import Bank of the U.S., November 8, 2013

[2] "Like it or not, coal is here to stay for a long time to come.Coal is abundant and geopolitically secure, and coal-fired plants are easily integrated into existing power systems."
—Maria van der Hoeven, the International Energy Agency's executive director, Paris Presentation of the IEA's Medium-Term Coal Market Report 2013, December 16, 2013

[3] According to Frank Clemente, a retired Pennsylvania State University professor, "Coal is the only fuel that can sustainably meet growing global demand at such a scale." *China has seen the future, and it is coal,* The Washington Post, December 30, 2010

[4] "By importing U.S. coal, China is not changing the amount of coal that it burns. I understand why on an emotional level people don't like it. But if you actually understand the economics, and you understand how climate change works, it's a non-issue." *Richard Morse, director of research on coal and carbon markets at Stanford University,* Trading Markets, December 27, 2010

[5] "Not all coal is created equal. The proposed export terminals in the Northwest would ship coal that is better for the environment in almost every way than the coal mined in East Asian countries like China, particularly with regard to sulfur dioxide and nitrogen oxide levels."*—Fred Thompson, professor of public management and policy at Willamette University, Exporting coal to China is the greenest option,* The Register-Guard, March 12, 2013

[6] "If Pacific Coast states construct sufficient coal export facilities, the United States is likely to sell heaps of coal to Asia in the years ahead, but that should cut—not raise—global emissions of greenhouse gases, according to Frank Wolak, professor of economics at Stanford University and director of Stanford's Program on Energy and Sustainable Development." *Reduce greenhouse gas by exporting coal? Yes, says Stanford economist,* The *Stanford Report,* January 15, 2013

[7] "This demand for coal in China appears to be long lived. The coal-fired power plants are expensive to build and are designed to last a long time, at least 30 years. If the United States does not build West Coast ports to ship western coal to Asia, Canada will likely do so." *Reduce greenhouse gas by exporting coal? Yes, says Stanford economist,* The *Stanford Report,* January 15, 2013

[8] Wood Mackenzie forecasts a worldwide coal demand growth of 5.5B tons from 2012 to 2030. [See also IEA data at *http://www.iea.org/aboutus/faqs/coal/*]

The U.S. Energy Information Administration (EIA) projects world energy consumption will increase 56 percent from 2013–2040.

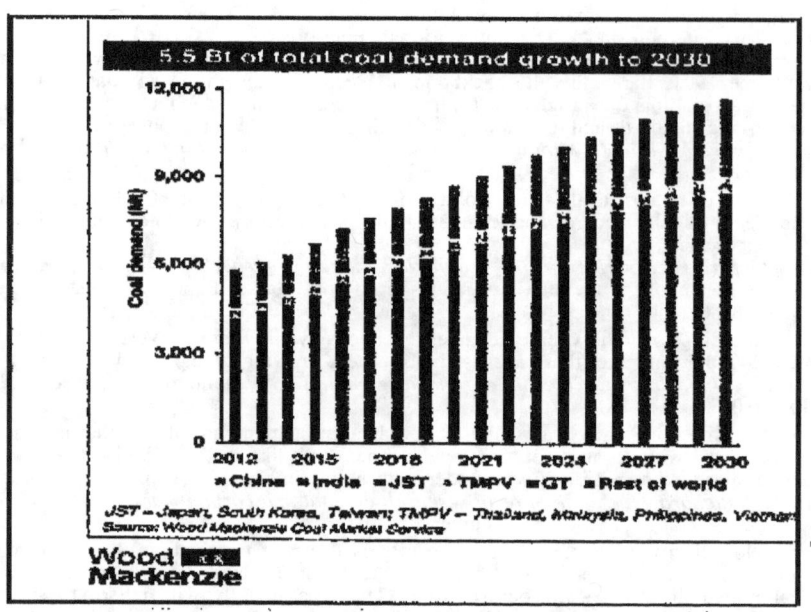

[9] Chapter PQ COAL QUALITY AND GEOCHEMISTRY, POWDER RIVER BASIN, WYOMING AND MONTANA, By G.D. Stricker and M.S. Ellis *in* U.S. Geological Survey Professional Paper 1625–A, 1999

Senator DAINES. Chairman Old Coyote, thank you.
Attorney General Fox.

STATEMENT OF HON. TIM FOX, ATTORNEY GENERAL, STATE OF MONTANA

Mr. FOX. Senator Daines, I'd like to thank you and Chairman Barrasso and Senator Tester for the invitation to speak here today. My name is Tim Fox. I'm the attorney general for the state of Montana.

I grew up in Hardin, and have a deep appreciation for the history, culture, but most importantly, the people of the Crow Nation.

Like most other Montanans, one thing the Crow people treasure is the land that they were born and raised in. I think the Chairman just alluded to that.

And thank you, Chairman Old Coyote, for hosting this important hearing.

Like most other Americans and Montanans, among the things that the Crow people would most like to see, for themselves and their children, are the opportunities for jobs that will allow them to make a reasonable living in the place they grew up so they can stay rather than having to move elsewhere of necessity.

The Crow Nation, like the rest of our state, is rich in resources. Those resources, including coal, are currently providing opportunity for Montanans, including the Crow people and, wisely used, will continue to do so.

I am concerned, though, that we are today seeing political and regulatory developments which, though not intentionally targeting the Crow Nation and, more generally, all of Montana, will, if unchecked, destroy present and future opportunities for our people.

I would like to talk briefly about a couple of those developments.

One of those developments is the U.S. Environmental Protection Agency's June 18, 2014 existing source proposal under Section 111(d) of the Clean Air Act.

I joined the attorney generals of 16 other states in comments on that proposal, but I also filed separate comments with Chairman Darrin Old Coyote of the Crow Nation, and I want to talk just a minute about those comments.

The Crow Nation's coal resources are still largely undeveloped, but there is currently one operating mine, the Absaloka Mine. And just that one mine provides two-thirds of the Crow Nation's annual non-federal budget, and is by far the largest private employer on the reservation.

Unfortunately, one of the very likely effects of the EPA's existing source rule would be to kill the market for the coal produced by the Absaloka Mine, which is nearly all sold to Minnesota utilities. This will, in turn, kill the mine, causing drastic loss of services and employment on the Crow Reservation.

The EPA has a legal duty under Executive Order 13175 to ensure meaningful and timely input by tribal officials in the development of regulatory proposals that affect tribes.

In the development of its existing source rule proposal, EPA went through the motions, issuing two, ''Dear Tribal Leader'' form letters, but nobody from the agency contacted the Crow Nation directly in a government-to-government contact saying, ''Excuse me, but this proposal could, as implemented in the State of Minnesota, kill the market for the output from the Absaloka Mine, and we'd like to talk to you about that.''

The Executive Order requires that the EPA ensure meaningful and timely input. The agency didn't get that job done before it promulgated its proposal, and the agency needs to withdraw the proposal and do the consultation it is required to do with the people of the Crow Nation.

The second development I wanted to talk about is the importance of keeping open the avenues of interstate commerce which coal mined in Montana needs to travel to reach markets outside our state, and this affects not only the Absaloka Mine in Crow Nation, but the other coal mines in Montana, both present and future.

As a landlocked state, we are dependent on port facilities in our sister states for shipping Montana-produced bulk commodity products to international markets.

There is currently an international market for coal mined in the northern Powder River Basin, and some coal is, in fact, being exported from Montana mines to that market.

For example, 4.7 million tons of coal was shipped in 2013 from the Spring Creek Mine through Westshore Terminals in British Columbia. But that terminal is at capacity, meaning more port capacity is needed to ensure open markets for our coal.

There are three active proposals to construct terminals which would provide capacity for shipment of coal from the northern Powder River Basin to international markets, two in the state of Washington, and one in Oregon.

The two in Washington, the Millennium Terminal Project at Longview and the Gateway Pacific Terminal at Cherry Point, are in the permit review and environmental analysis stage.

The Coyote Island Terminal project in Oregon, which would provide a terminal to take coal from rail at Boardman, Oregon for transport by barge down the Columbia to Port Westward for loadout onto ocean-going vessels, was denied a fill permit by the Oregon Department of State Lands, and an administrative appeal of that decision is pending.

My office has been involved in the scoping process for the environmental analysis of the Gateway Pacific Project, and we are actively tracking the process for that Millennium Project.

We have actually intervened in the appeal of the permit denial for the Coyote Island Terminal, along with the state of Wyoming.

The reason we have taken these steps is to ensure, as our sister states make their decisions regarding these port proposals, that our state's constitutional right not to have the avenues of interstate commence unduly burdened is fully protected.

I know from discussions I have had with Chairman Old Coyote, that the Crow Nation shares these concerns.

As I mentioned a minute ago, one of the effects of the EPA's proposed existing source rule would be to close the power plants which are the market for the Absaloka Mine, and with that possibility looming, the Asian market is the obvious alternative market for coal from that mine. But our coal can't reach those markets without suitable port facilities in our sister states.

This is a very big concern to our state and for the Crow Nation. For the year 2013, the tax revenues collected by the state of Montana on coal mined in Montana totaled $78,134,000. I have already told you of the economic benefits the Absaloka Mine provides to the Crow Nation.

As domestic markets for Montana and Crow coal are diminished by the impacts of political trends and federal regulatory initiatives, access to international markets in Asia will become critical to the economic welfare of our state and the Crow Nation.

Senator Daines, thank you again for giving me some time here today. Thank you again, Mr. Chairman.

I want to thank my classmate, Doctor Yarlott, for hosting this hearing at Little Big Horn College.

And I say hello to my friends in the Crow Nation and thank you for listening to me, and I would be happy to answer any questions you may have.

Thank you.

[The prepared statement of Mr. Fox follows:]

PREPARED STATEMENT OF HON. TIM FOX, ATTORNEY GENERAL, STATE OF MONTANA

Senator Daines, members of the Committee, thank you for inviting me to speak here today. I'm Tim Fox, attorney general of the State of Montana.

I grew up in Hardin, and have a deep appreciation for the history, culture, but most important, the people of the Crow Nation. Like most other Montanans, one thing the Crow people treasure is the land they were born and raised in. And like most other Montanans, among the things they would most like to see, for themselves and their children, are opportunities for jobs that will allow them to make a reasonable living in the place they grew up, so they can stay rather than having to move elsewhere of necessity.

The Crow Nation, like the rest of our State, is rich in resources. Those resources, including coal, are currently providing opportunity for Montanans, including the Crow people, and, wisely used, will continue to do so. I am concerned, though, that we are today seeing political and regulatory developments which, though not intentionally targeting the Crow Nation and, more generally, all of Montana, will, if unchecked, destroy present and future opportunities for our people. I would like to talk briefly about a couple of those developments.

One of those developments is the U.S. Environmental Protection Agency's June 18, 2014 existing source proposal under section 111(d) of the Clean Air Act. I joined the attorneys general of sixteen other states in comments on that proposal, but I also filed separate comments with Chairman Darrin Old Coyote of the Crow Nation, and I want to talk just a minute about those comments.

The Crow Nation's coal resources are still largely undeveloped, but there is currently one operating mine, the Absaloka Mine, and just that one mine provides two-thirds of the Crow Nation's annual non-federal budget, and is by far the largest private employer on the reservation.

Unfortunately, one of the very likely effects of EPA's existing source rule would be to kill the market for the coal produced by the Absaloka Mine, which is nearly all sold to Minnesota utilities. This will in turn kill the mine, causing drastic loss of services and employment on the Crow Reservation.

EPA has a legal duty under Executive Order 13175 to ensure meaningful and timely input by tribal officials in the development of regulatory proposals that affect tribes. In the development of its existing source rule proposal, EPA went through the motions, issuing two "Dear Tribal Leader" form letters, but nobody from the agency contacted the Crow Nation directly in a government-to-government contact, saying, "excuse me, but this proposal could, as implemented in the State of Minnesota, kill the market for the output from the Absaloka Mine, and we'd like to talk to you about that." The executive Order requires that EPA "ensure" meaningful and timely input. The agency didn't get that job done before it promulgated its proposal, and the agency needs to withdraw the proposal and do the consultation it is required to do.

The second development I wanted to talk about is the importance of keeping open the avenues of interstate commerce which coal mined in Montana needs to travel to reach markets outside our State. As a landlocked state, we are dependent on port facilities in our sister states for shipping Montana-produced bulk commodity products to international markets. There is currently an international market for coal mined in the Northern Powder River Basin, and some coal is in fact being exported from Montana mines to that market. For example 4.7 million tons of coal was shipped in 2013 from the Spring Creek Mine, through Westshore Terminals in British Columbia. But that terminal is at capacity, meaning more port capacity is needed to ensure open markets for our coal.

There are three active proposals to construct terminals which would provide capacity for shipment of coal from the Northern Powder River Basin to international markets, two in the State of Washington, and one in Oregon. The two in Washington, the Millenium Terminal Project at Longview and the Gateway Pacific Terminal at Cherry Point, are in the permit review and environmental analysis stage. The Coyote Island Terminal project in Oregon, which would provide a terminal to take coal from rail at Boardman, Oregon, for transport by barge down the Columbia to Port Westward for loadout onto ocean-going vessels, was denied a fill permit by the Oregon Department of State Lands, and an administrative appeal of that decision is pending.

My office has been involved in the scoping process for the environmental analysis of the Gateway Pacific Project and we are actively tracking the process for the Millenium Project. We have actually intervened in the appeal of the permit denial for the Coyote Island Terminal, along with the State of Wyoming. The reason we have taken these steps is to ensure, as our sister states make their decisions regarding these port proposals, that our State's constitutional right not to have the avenues of interstate commerce unduly burdened is fully protected.

I know from discussions I have had with Chairman Old Coyote, that the Crow Nation shares these concerns. As I mentioned a minute ago, one of the effects of EPA's proposed existing source rule would be to close the power plants which are the market for the Absaloka Mine, and with that possibility looming, the Asian market is the obvious alternative market for coal from that mine. But our coal can't reach those markets without suitable port facilities in our sister states.

This is a very big concern to our State and for the Crow Nation. For the year 2013, the tax revenues collected by the State of Montana on coal mined in Montana totaled $78,134,334. I have already told you of the economic benefits the Absaloka Mine provides to the Crow Nation. As domestic markets for Montana and Crow coal are diminished by the impacts of political trends and federal regulatory initiatives, access to international markets in Asia will become critical to the economic welfare of our State and the Crow Nation.

Senator Daines, members of the committee, thank you again for giving me some time here today to speak on behalf of the people of Montana. I'm happy to answer any questions you may have.

Senator DAINES. Thank you, Attorney General Fox.
Speaker Lorenzo Bates.

STATEMENT OF HON. LORENZO BATES, SPEAKER, NAVAJO NATION COUNCIL; ACCOMPANIED BY RAYMOND SMITH, JR., COUNCIL DELEGATE

Mr. BATES. Good morning. My name is Lorenzo Bates. I'm the Speaker of the Navajo Nation Council currently serving in my fourth term as Council Delegate, and representing the communities of Nenahnezad, Newcomb, San Juan, Tiis Tsoh Sikaad, Tse'Daa'Kaan and Upper Fruitland.

I stand before you today representing these communities. These communities are directly impacted by the coal economy as well as the Navajo Nation as a whole whose future is dependent on this natural resource.

I want first to extend my gratitude, on behalf of the Navajo Nation to Chairman Barrasso, Vice-Chairman Tester, Senator Daines and the members of the Senate Committee on Indian Affairs for holding this Oversight Field Hearing on Empowering Indian Country, as well as my brothers and sisters of the Crow Nation for hosting these very important talks today.

I am currently serving my 13th year as a Navajo Nation elected official, having previously served as Chairman of the Navajo Nation Budget and Finance Committee.

I am deeply grateful to have this opportunity to address you here today with this past experience as my guide, as well as a guide for the Navajo Nation in our future, despite the many challenges that face us as we strive to empower our Nation through self-determination and the natural resources given to us by the Great Creator.

The Navajo Nation is a sovereign nation located in the Four Corners region of the United States, encompassing over 27,425 square miles and occupying land in the states of Utah, Arizona and New Mexico.

Of the 500 recognized tribes and 318 reservations, the Navajo Nation is the largest, with a population topping 300,000, and is larger in land mass than 10 of the 50 states.

The Navajo Nation Government is balanced between three branches, including the Executive Branch with a President and Vice-president, who are elected by the Navajo people; the Legislative branch, with a Navajo Nation Council; five Standing Committees; a Speaker; 24 elected officials, representing 110 communities, who serve on a committee; and the Judicial Branch with a Chief Justice and Supreme Court.

Of the 300,000 members of the Navajo Nation, less than half are able to make a living on the Nation, with the others choosing to move to one of the larger cities for work. Our unemployment rate is well over 50 percent and growing with our population as economic development remains stagnate.

We currently graduate over 2,000 high school graduates each year while creating an average of 40 new jobs resulting in dire circumstances.

Currently our General Funds represents one-third of our overall budget. For 2015, it was at $175 million, with approximately 60 percent of that produced from our coal economy. The remainder of our budget is comprised of external funds, including the federal, which control up to 43 percent.

We recently collaborated with the School of Business at Arizona State University to study the economic impact of one of our two coal mines on the Navajo Nation economy.

What we found is that our Peabody Coal Mine, together with our Navajo Generating Station will boost the Navajo Nation economy by over $13 billion over the next 25 years.

That is just the economic benefits to the Navajo. It does not include the economic linkage enjoyed by surrounding communities off our reservation.

Our 2010 Comprehensive Economic Development Strategy uncovered the fact that 64 percent of every dollar generated on the Navajo Nation is spent off the reservation due to the lack of retail outlets located within our Nation.

The Navajo Nation economy is often compared to as a third world country. Speaking before the Navajo Nation Council on January 18, 1996, Senator John McCain made the following statement:

". . . Each of us shares a strong commitment to promote and defend tribal sovereignty, tribal self-governance, and tribal self-sufficiency.

But my friends, these things we hold dear, will wither and die unless they are watered by a strong reservation economy that produces a decent standard of living for all our people. Unfortunately, as you well know, economic development success stories in Indian Country are still the exception and not the rule.

Most Americans would be stunned to find out that the basic necessities of life they take for granted are solely lacking on the Navajo Reservation and in many other Native American communities across the Country. No other group of Americans is more economically depressed than Native Americans, and no other areas in America suffer more from inadequate infrastructure and a lack of job opportunities than do Indian Reservations and Alaska Native villages.

Here at Navajo, your large land-base and membership magnify the socio-economic problems that infect much of Indian Country. In my lifetime I have been too many places around the world and have experienced many terrible living conditions. What is so shocking is that the social and economic conditions for many Navajos closely resemble those of people living in Third World countries."

With our high unemployment rate, our lack of income, paved roads, modern housing; lower education level; our high poverty rate, give our Navajo economy such a resemblance.

The Navajo Nation has identified four main areas of focus within our Navajo Nation Energy Policy as it relates to the energy needs of the nation, which will guide decisions during the 23rd Navajo Nation Council.

One, first is to protect and expand upon the current jobs and revenues realized by our current energy projects located on the Navajo Nation.

Next is to expand and diversify our energy portfolio and transition our energy production into alternative and renewable resources to meet the future needs of our people.

Another area of focus is to ensure that the Navajo people have access to residential and commercial electricity here at home and with competitive rates.

Last, but certainly not least, is to strive to keep our balance with Mother Nature and the needs of our people. With these guiding principles, the Navajo Nation will make decisions that are responsible and meet the needs of our Navajo people.

The Navajo Nation mines approximately 8 to 10 million tons of coal each year, down from 13 to 16 million tons before the U.S. EPA regulations began to take its toll on our resources, and we have billions of tons more to mine to feed our Navajo economy.

Additionally, we produce approximately 3,750 megawatts of electricity sold primarily off our Nation, effectively taking advantage of hydroelectricity from the Glen Canyon Dam to meet our Nation's needs.

This industry is responsible for more than 2,000 of the highest paying jobs on the Navajo Nation and better than 60 percent of our general revenues. These revenues represent our ability to act as a sovereign nation and to meet our own needs without a handout through outside jurisdictions.

It is unthinkable to consider what our people would do without these critical funds. In fact, our reliance on these resources has led us to invest in the purchase of our Navajo mine from BHP this past year to gain greater control of our resources and insure the continuation of these vital funds for our future generations.

This purchase was made through our Navajo Transitional Energy Company, who, as its name suggests, is mandated to transition our Nation into our energy future by investing no less than 10 percent of its profits into alternative and renewable energy development.

The consequences of the latest rounds of EPA regulations resulted in the shutdown of three of the five power generating units at the Four Corners Power Plant and the forced investment of a billion dollars in BART retrofits on the remaining two units.

This, in turn, reduced the coal mined at our Navajo mine while simultaneously increasing the cost of power generation.

The Four Corners Power Plant and the Navajo mine were poised to discontinue operation this year if it were not for the Navajo Nation's purchase of the Navajo mine.

While we are now in a position to maintain our jobs and revenues and possibly increase them from this mine, we are being threatened by additional EPA regulations and an unstable energy future.

Across the United States, coal economies are feeling the pinch, but not near to the extent as the Navajo Nation. What other economy in the United States stands to lose as much?

Some may call this a war on coal, but from the Navajo Nation's perspective, this is a war on the Navajo economy and our ability to act as a sovereign nation.

It is difficult enough working to meet the needs of the Navajo Nation with our current resources. I do not dare imagine the difficulty that will come with a 50 percent reduction in general revenues due to our coal mines shutting down. With our current budget heavily subsidized by federal funds, this scenario only increases that dependence.

Many coal critics have argued that we can simply convert our power generation to natural gas and renewable energy while maintaining our jobs and revenues.

Similar arguments were made when the Mohave Generating Station in Nevada shut down in 2005 cutting our coal supply through the Black Mesa pipeline, and we have yet, we have yet to see any replacement of those jobs or revenue ten years later.

The challenges of economically producing power through gas at the high elevations common on Navajo are enough to discourage the investment.

Navajo is open to solar generation, although it takes 10 acres per megawatt to produce commercial power and has yet to significantly meet market demand.

Even if these resources were cut, we would still see major economic cuts as our coal mines would shut down, which represents over, again, 50 percent of our jobs and revenues realized through coal power generation.

The challenges are daunting when we look to the future of our Navajo people. Our hope lies in the understanding and collaboration of the U.S. government to insure that the transition of our Nation's energy resources happens in an economically responsible way, considerate of the lives that are impacted by the policies written by individuals who have yet to visit our Nation.

We continue to request for government-to-government consultation that is on equal ground, cognizant of our needs and not merely a box to be checked off on yet another government form.

Our hope lies in the development of alternative clean technologies that would effectively bridge the gap between the utilization of our coal resources and the environmental concerns of the day.

We implore the U.S. government to work with us to develop the financial incentives necessary for investors to bring these coal technologies to our reservation where our need is so great, where we have a ready workforce, abundant coal resources, and the infrastructure to get gasified coal products and captured carbon into the market.

The Navajo Nation wants to be a part of the solution that brings the United States closer to energy independence while meeting our needs at home.

We ask that the U.S. government respect the decisions we make with our state, tribal and regional partners in response to meeting our ever changing environmental regulations while maintaining our regional and tribal economies.

When we are able to work together in a meaningful way we can find some middle ground when it comes to our financial stability as a nation.

We want to move forward towards self-reliance by utilizing our resources that meet our needs while reducing our dependence on external funds from the Federal Government.

In conclusion, I would like to reiterate the tremendous need to work together to meet the needs of our people and not to take the easy road in implementing federal standards at the peril of local tribal economies.

Take the time to listen, to truly listen, and understand our needs and to work with us to find creative solutions to the challenges of our day.

Allow us the financial incentives necessary to achieve the realization of basic necessities, such as home ownership, electricity, water, access to improved roads and an education for our children so that they may be in a position to do what we are unable to do.

An education that will allow them to participate in the transition of our energy resources and the financial know-how to compete in the worldwide marketplace.

I thank you.

And with your permission, I would like to have my colleague, Mr. Raymond Smith, sitting next to me, provide us with additional remarks in addition to what I presented here.

Mr. SMITH. Good morning.

Senator DAINES. Good morning.

Mr. SMITH. Thank you, Senator.

My name is Raymond Smith, Jr. I'm from the Navajo Nation as a Council Delegate.

I'd just like to bring up a couple of keynotes that our Nation is experiencing with the coal intrusion.

We're having technical difficulties—

Senator DAINES. Excuse me, I think what we'll have to do with the time is I'll have you submit your comments as written record, and have them recorded as part of written testimony, but I'm going to have to keep moving ahead here with these other witnesses for the time management.

So, if you could just submit those in a written record. Would that be okay?

Mr. SMITH. That's fine with me.

Senator DAINES. Okay. Thank you very much for your understanding. I appreciate it.

The prepared statement of Mr. Bates follows:]

PREPARED STATEMENT OF HON. LORENZO BATES, SPEAKER, NAVAJO NATION COUNCIL

Good Morning. My name is Lorenzo C. Bates, Speaker of the 23rd Navajo Nation Council currently serving in my fourth term as Council Delegate representing the communities of; Nenahnezad, Newcomb, San Juan, Tiis Tsoh Sikaad, Tse'Daa'Kaan and Upper Fruitland. I stand before you today representing these communities that are directly impacted by the coal economy as well as the Navajo Nation as a whole whose future is dependent on this natural resource.

I first want to extend my gratitude, on behalf of the Navajo Nation to Chairman Barrasso, Vice-Chairman Tester, Senator Daines and the members of the Senate

Committee on Indian Affairs for holding this Oversight Field Hearing on Empowering Indian Country, as well as my brothers and sisters of the Crow Nation for hosting these very important talks.

I am currently serving in my 13th year as a Navajo Nation elected official having previously served as Chairman of the Navajo Nation Budget and finance Committee. I am deeply grateful to have this opportunity to address you here today with this past experience as my guide and the hope we as a Nation have in our future, despite the many challenges that face us as we strive to empower our Nation through Self-Determination and the natural resources given to us by the Great Creator.

The Navajo Nation is a sovereign Nation located in the Four Corners region of the United States, encompassing over 27,425 Square Miles and occupying land in the States of Utah, Arizona and New Mexico. Of the 500 recognized tribes and 318 reservations, the Navajo Nation is the largest with a population topping 300,000 and is larger in land mass than 10 of the 50 states.

The Navajo Nation Government is balanced between three branches including the Executive Branch with a President and Vice President who are elected by the Navajo people, the Legislative Branch with a Navajo Nation Council, five Standing Committees a Speaker and 24 elected Council Delegates representing 110 Navajo communities who each serve on a Committee and the Judicial Branch with a Chief Justice and Supreme Court. Of the 300 thousand members of the Navajo Nation, less than half are able to make a living on the Nation with the others choosing to move to one of the larger cities for work. Our unemployment rate is over 50 percent and growing with our population as economic development remains stagnate. We currently graduate over 2,000 high school graduates each year while creating an average of 40 new jobs resulting in dire circumstances. Currently, our General Funds represent ⅓ of our overall budget at $175 million with approximately 60 percent of that produced from our coal economy. The remainder of our budget is comprised of external funds from the federal government. We recently collaborated with the W.P. Carey School of Business at Arizona State University to study the economic impact of one of our two coal mines on the Navajo Nation economy. What we found is that our Peabody Coal mine together with our Navajo Generating Station will boost the Navajo Nation economy by over $13 billion dollars over the next 25 years! That is just the economic benefits to Navajo and does not include the economic leakage enjoyed by the surrounding communities off our reservation. Our 2010 Comprehensive Economic Development Strategy uncovered the fact that 64 percent of every dollar generated on the Navajo Nation is spent off the reservation due to the lack of retail outlets located within our Nation.

The Navajo economy is often compared to as a third world country. Speaking before the Navajo Nation Council on January 18, 1996, Senator John McCain made the following statement:

". . . Each of us shares a strong commitment to promote and defend tribal sovereignty, tribal self-governance, and tribal self-sufficiency.

But my friends, these things we hold dear, will wither and die unless they are watered by a strong Reservation economy that produces a decent standard of living for all our people. Unfortunately, as you well know, economic development success stories in Indian Country are still the exception and not the rule. Most Americans would be stunned to find out that the basic necessities of life they take for granted are solely lacking on the Navajo Reservation and in many other Native American communities across the Country. No other group of Americans is more economically depressed than Native Americans, and no other areas in America suffer more from inadequate infrastructure and a lack of job opportunities than do Indian Reservations and Alaska Native villages.

Here at Navajo, your large land-base and membership magnify the destitution and socio-economic problems that infect much of Indian Country. In my lifetime I have been too many places around the world and have experienced many terrible living conditions. What is so shocking is that the social and economic conditions for many Navajos closely resemble those of people living in Third World countries."

With our high unemployment rate; our lack of income, paved roads, modern housing and amenities; lower education level; our high poverty rate; give our Navajo economy such a resemblance.

The Navajo Nation has identified four main areas of focus within our Navajo Nation Energy Policy as it relates to the energy needs of the Navajo Nation, which will guide my decisions during my time as Speake of the 23rd Navajo Nation Council; first is to protect and expand upon the current jobs and revenues realized by our current energy projects located on the Navajo Nation; nest is to expand and diversify our energy portfolio and transition our energy production into alternative and renewable sources to meet the future needs of our people; another area of focus is to ensure that the Navajo people have access to residential and commercial electricity here at home and within competitive rates; last but certainly not least is to strive to keep our balance with Mother Nature and the needs of our people. With these guiding principles the Navajo Nation will make decisions that are responsible and meet the needs of our Navajo people.

The Navajo Nation mines approximately 8 to 10 million tons of coal each year, down from 13 to 16 million tons before the U.S. EPA regulations began to take its toll on our resources and we have billions of tons more to mine to feed our Navajo economy. Additionally, we produce approximately 3,750 Megawatts of electricity sold primarily off our Nation, effectively taking advantage of hydroelectricity from the Glen Canyon Dam to meet our Nation's needs. This industry is responsible for more than 2,000 of the highest paying jobs on the Navajo Nation and better than 60 percent of our General Revenues. These revenues represent our ability to act as a sovereign nation and meet our own needs without a hand out to outside jurisdictions. It is unthinkable to consider what our people would do without these critical funds. In fact, our reliance on these resources has led us to invest in the purchase of our Navajo Mine from BHP this past year to gain greater control of our resources and insure the continuation of these vital funds for our future generations. This purchase was made through our Navajo Transitional Energy Company, who, as its name suggests is mandated to transition our Nation into our energy future by investing no less than 10 percent of its profits into alternative and renewable energy development. The consequences of the latest rounds of EPA regulations resulted in the shutdown of three of the five power generating units at the Four Corners Power Plant and the forced investment of a billion dollars in BART retrofits on the remaining two units. This in turn reduced the coal mined at our Navajo Mine while simultaneously increasing the cost of power generation. With the economies of scale lost to circumstance, the Four Corners Power Plant and the Navajo Mine were poised to discontinue operation this year if it were not for our purchase of Navajo Mine. While we are now in a position to maintain our jobs and revenues and possibly increase them from this mine, we are being threatened by additional EPA regulations and an unstable energy future. Across the United States, coal economies are feeling the pinch, but not near to the extent as the Navajo Nation, what other economy in the United States stands to lose as much? Some may call this a war on coal, but from the Navajo Nations perspective, this is a war on the Navajo economy and our ability to act as a sovereign Nation.

It is difficult enough working to meet the needs of the Navajo Nation with our current resources; I do not dare imagine the difficulty that would come with a 50 percent reduction in general revenues due to our coal mines shutting down! With our current budget heavily subsidized by federal funds, this scenario only increases that dependence. Many coal critics have argued that we can simply convert our power generation to natural gas and renewable energy while maintaining our jobs and revenues. Similar arguments were made when the Mohave Generating Station in Nevada shut down in 2005 cutting our coal supply through our Black Mesa Pipeline and we have yet to see any replacement jobs or revenue ten years later. The challenges of economically producing power through gas at the high elevations common on Navajo are enough to discourage the investment. Navajo is open to solar generation although it takes 10 acres per Megawatt to produce commercial power and has yet to sufficiently meet market demand. Even if these resources were possible, we would still see major economic cuts as our coal mines would shut down which represents over 50 percent of our jobs and revenues realized through coal power generation.

The challenges are daunting when we look to the future of our Navajo people, our hope lies in the understanding and collaboration of the U.S. Government to insure that the transition of our Nation's energy resources happens in an economically responsible way, considerate of the lives that are impacted by policies written by individuals who have yet to visit our Nation. We continue to request for government to government consultation that is on equal ground, cognizant of our needs and not merely a box to be checked off on yet another government form. Our hope lies in the development of alternative clean coal technologies that would effectively bridge the gap between the utilization of our coal resources and the environmental concerns of the day. We implore the US Government to work with us to develop the financial incentives necessary for investors to bring these clean coal technologies to our reservations where the need is so great, where we have a ready workforce, abundant coal resources and the infrastructure to get gasified coal products and captured carbon into the market. The Navajo Nation wants to be a part of the solution that brings the United States closer to energy independence while meeting our needs at home. We ask that the US Government respect the decisions we make with our State, tribal and regional partners in response to meeting the ever changing environmental regulations while maintaining our regional and tribal economies. When we are able to work together in a meaningful way we can find some middle ground when it comes to our financial stability as a Nation. We want to move towards self-reliance by utilizing our resources to meet our needs while reducing our dependence on external funds from the Federal Government.

In conclusion, I would like to reiterate the tremendous need to work together to meet the needs of our people and not to take the easy road in implementing federal standards at the peril of local tribal economies. Take the time to truly listen and understand our needs and work with us to find creative solutions to the challenges of our day. Allow us the financial incentives necessary to achieve the realization of basic necessities such as home ownership, electricity, water, access to improved roads and an education for our children so that they may be in a position to do what we are unable to. An education that will allow them to participate in the transition of our energy resources and the financial know how to compete in the worldwide marketplace.

Senator DAINES. Mr. Small.

STATEMENT OF JASON SMALL, JOURNEYMAN BOILERMAKER; LABOR ADVOCATE; AND NORTHERN CHEYENNE TRIBAL MEMBER

Mr. SMALL. Good morning, Senator Daines and members of the Committee.

My name is Jason Small. I am an enrolled member of the Northern Cheyenne Tribe, and I'm also a resident on the reservation. I am a journeyman boilermaker, a member of Boilermaker Local 11 here in Montana.

And my comments today are based upon my experience working in coal-related employment across the nation in the capacity as a journeyman welder, boilermaker and also a union steward.

I am also one of two internationally certified welding instructors here in Montana for the boilermakers. I teach at the Spencer Benson Welding Trading Center at Colstrip, quite frequently, and it assists many young people, especially members of the Crow and the Northern Cheyenne Tribes to enter the boilermaker trade. That center is financially supported by the International Brotherhood of Boilermakers and also PP&L.

So, first, I'd like to thank you, Senator, for arranging this hearing, specifically asking how the Congress can be more helpful to tribes, such as the Crow and the Navajo, who are developing coal resources, and the Northern Cheyenne, who will hopefully pursue this option to address unacceptable rates of unemployment and poverty on our reservation.

As you know, Indian Reservations contain 30 percent of the nation's coal reserves west of the Mississippi, and also $1.5 trillion of energy resources. In my opinion, coal must continue to be the mainstay in the energy mix.

While wind, solar, bio-mass, and hydroelectricity can contribute to our national energy needs, it is clear that they cannot totally replace coal as a base load power source.

I am a strong proponent for development of the rich Northern Cheyenne coal reserves, recently expressing my reasons in a widely publicized Op-Ed piece.

While development is opposed by some, I firmly believe that a majority of the tribal members are favorably inclined. So do some of our traditional leaders, such as Tim Lame Woman, who is the

General District Chairperson for the reservation, and he's also a direct descendant of Chief Little Wolf and a member of the traditional Elkhorn Scrapers Society.

Our Tribal President Llevando "Cowboy" Fisher promised to hold a referendum vote on that question, and I believe it will overwhelmingly pass. In a 1990s vote, the majority of the tribal members have already said "yes" to coal development.

I believe the main reason it will pass, in my opinion, is because of the positive experiences that the Northern Cheyenne have had at Colstrip, through employment and other financial benefits from agreements related to Units 3 and 4 and the Western Energy Coal Mine.

Presently, about 125 tribal members are employed at PP&L generating stations and the mine. Many others have retired and are now enjoying a good retirement income that come from these sorts of jobs.

And you have to realize that the people who are still working there draw some of the highest hourly wages in the state and are thus able to provide very well for their immediate families and often extended family members.

This employment, which started in the 1980s, has significantly changed the attitudes of many Northern Cheyenne about coal development because it has enabled them to break out of poverty.

In addition, those companies provide scholarships, charitable donations and support environmental air quality on the reservation to the tune of about $500,000 a year.

Over the years, the Cheyenne have learned about reclamation; developing confidence that the lands can be fully restored. Indeed, one of our tribal members actually heads up Western Energy's Reclamation Program.

Under federal and state law, the companies are held to very high standards, and many of the Cheyenne have learned that the lands disturbed by mining when reclaimed are actually in better condition than they were prior to mining.

Western Energy has received numerous national awards for reclamation excellence including the National Institute for Urban Wildlife. In addition to federal and state laws, the tribes can enact additional laws to protect sacred sites and address other tribal concerns related to reservation coal development.

The energy complexes at Colstrip and Crow provide profound benefits to the region, state and two reservations. For example, economists from the University of Montana provide the following statistics:

- The Colstrip generating plants provide 3,740 jobs directly related to energy production in Montana, 3500 in eastern Montana alone. An additional 2,688 private sector jobs are related also.

- Personal income from coal-related employment is nearly $363 million statewide.

- PP&L Colstrip employs 363 permanent workers also, which includes 41 tribal members, which is nearly one-eighth of the workforce.

- Others are also employed by subcontractors, especially during the outages and overhauls in the spring when there are 680 employed by North American Energy Services alone, and also many of those are Navajo workers that have a huge boilermaker constituency.
- The Western Energy Mine in Colstrip currently employs 80 minorities, and the majority of are them Northern Cheyenne, nearly one-third of the craft workforce. This satisfies an original agreement or an original tribal goal of developing a trained workforce for the day when the Northern Cheyenne would develop their own reserves.
- The beneficial impacts of the Westmoreland Mine at Crow are even more powerful, as Mr. Old Coyote here has already stated.

In conclusion, I suggest that responsible coal development can be a major key enabling the Northern Cheyenne and its members to rise out of poverty and achieve self-sufficiency.

Your national leadership and compassion for the native people is essential in this struggle. I ask you to please keep up the good fight, and particularly against the unrealistic and punitive regulations being pushed by the EPA.

We know that additional regulations will be mandated. They must be pursued in a reasonable manner, though, which will not devastate the economy of southeastern Montana and still allow for responsible development.

Thank you for the opportunity to testify, and I will be happy to answer any questions you may have.

[The prepared statement of Mr. Small follows:]

PREPARED STATEMENT OF JASON SMALL, JOURNEYMAN BOILERMAKER; LABOR ADVOCATE; AND NORTHERN CHEYENNE TRIBAL MEMBER

Senator Daines and members of the Committee: My name is Jason Small. I am an enrolled member of the Northern Cheyenne Tribe and reside on the Northern Cheyenne Reservation. I am also a journeyman boilermaker, member of Montana's Local 11, and my comments today are based upon my experience working in coal-related employment across the Nation, including as a union steward. I am also one of two internationally certified welding instructors in Montana. I teach at the Spencer Benson Welding Training Center, Colstrip, MT which assists many young people, especially members of the Crow and Northern Cheyenne Tribes to enter the boilermaker trade. That center is financially supported by the International Brotherhood of Boilermakers and PPL as a way to help people gain a trade, particularly those from the Cheyenne Reservation with 70 percent unemployment.

Thank you Senator for arranging this hearing, specifically asking how the Congress can be more helpful to Tribes such as the Crow and Navajo who are developing coal resources and the Northern Cheyenne who will hopefully pursue this option to address unacceptable rates of unemployment and poverty on our Reservation. *As you probably know, Indian Reservations contain 30 percent of the nation's coal reserves west of the Mississippi, an estimated 1.5 trillion dollars of energy resources.* In my opinion, coal must continue to be the mainstay in the energy mix. While wind, solar, bio-mass, and hydro energy can contribute to our national energy needs, it is clear they cannot totally replace coal as a base load power sources.

I am a strong proponent for development of the rich Northern Cheyenne coal reserves, recently expressing my reasons in widely publicized Op-Ed piece. While development is opposed by some, I firmly believe that a majority of tribal members are favorable inclined. So do some of our traditional leaders such as Tim Lame Woman, General District Chairperson for the Reservation, a direct descendant of Chief Little Wolf and member of the traditional Elkhorn Scrapers Society . Tribal President Llevando "Cowboy" Fisher promised to hold a referendum vote on that question and I believe it will overwhelmingly pass. In a 1990's vote, the majority of tribal members said "Yes" to coal development, but "No" to coal bed methane. Still, our current leaders feel that another vote is necessary.

The main reason it will pass, in my opinion, is because of the positive experiences that the Northern Cheyenne have had at Colstrip, through employment and other financial benefits from agreements related to Units 3 & 4 and the Western Energy Coal Mine. Presently, about 125 tribal members are employed at PPL Generating Stations and the mine. Many others have retired, now enjoying good retirement income. Those employees draw some of the highest hourly wages in the State and are thus able to provide very well for their immediate families and often extended family members. This employment which started in the 1980's has significantly changed the attitudes of many Northern Cheyenne about coal development because it has enabled them to break out of poverty. In addition, those companies provide scholarships, charitable donations and support environmental air quality on the Reservation to the tune of about $500,000 per year. Over a hundred other tribal members have gained college degrees as a result of the PPL and Western Energy scholarship programs.

Over the years, the Cheyenne have learned about reclamation, developing confidence that the lands can be fully restored. Indeed Rich Spang, a great-great grandson of one our most famous Chiefs, Dull Knife heads up Western Energy's Reclamation Program. Under federal and state law, the companies are held to very high standards and many of the Cheyenne have learned that the lands disturbed by mining when reclaimed are actually in better condition than pre-mining. The water comes back; the grazing is prime, with all of the traditional plants re-introduced and the reclaimed lands is prime wildlife habitat. Western has received numerous national awards for reclamation excellence including the National Institute for Urban Wildlife. In addition to federal and state laws, Tribes can enact additional law to protect sacred sites and address other tribal concerns related to reservation coal development.

The energy complexes at Colstrip and at Crow provide profound benefits to the region, State and two Reservations. For example, economists from University of Montana provide the following statistics:

- The Colstrip generating plants provide 3,740 jobs directly related to energy production in Montana, 3,500 in eastern Montana. An additional 2,688 private sector jobs are related.
- Personal income from coal-related employment is about 363 million.
- PPL Colstrip employs 363 permanent workers, including 41 tribal members, one-eighth of the workforce. Others are employed by subcontractors, including during the annual overhaul when 680 are employed by North American Energy Services alone including many Navajo boilermakers.
- The Western Energy Mine, Colstrip currently employs 80 minorities, the majority Northern Cheyenne, nearly one-third of the craft workforce. This satisfies an original tribal goal of developing a trained work force for the day when the Northern Cheyenne would develop their own reserves.
- The beneficial impacts of the Westmoreland Mine at Crow are even more powerful and I leave that discussion to Chairman Old Coyote.

In conclusion, I suggest that responsible coal development can be a major key enabling the Northern Cheyenne Tribe and its members to rise out of poverty and achieve self-sufficiency. Your national leadership and compassion for the native people is essential in this struggle. Please keep up the good fight, particularly with the unrealistic and punitive regulations being pushed by EPA. While know, that additional regulations will be mandated, they must be pursued in a reasonable manner which will not devastate the economy of southeastern Montana and still allow for responsible development.

Thank you for the opportunity to testify. I will be happy to answer any questions you may have.

Senator DAINES. Thank you, Mr. Small. Mr. Henson.

ERIC HENSON, SENIOR VICE PRESIDENT, COMPASS LEXECON; RESEARCH AFFILIATE, HARVARD PROJECT ON AMERICAN INDIAN ECONOMIC DEVELOPMENT

Mr. HENSON. Thank you.

Thank you, Senator Daines, for holding this hearing, and thank you, Chairman, for inviting us all to tribal land.

To be brief, my name is Eric Henson, a member of the Chickasaw Nation, and I think that most people here know, I work a couple of jobs.

I work at an economics consulting firm and we did a study about a year ago on the importance of coal development on the Crow Nation.

I also work as a Research Fellow at the Harvard Project on American Indian Economic Development, and I have had the great privilege to be associated with the Harvard Project for about 18 years now.

There are studies in my written comments, but keep in mind the principle, and you'll find that continued and expanded coal production on Crow lands represents up to $360 to $370 million a year to the state economy, more than a thousand jobs, tens of millions of dollars in local, state and federal taxes, and most importantly, from our perspective, the potential quadrupling of the non-federal funds for the Crow Tribe.

This would be a major benefit for the tribe, to maintain and achieve a massive amount of self-sufficiency that it has so far been unable to achieve.

As you've heard, the socio-economic conditions at the Crow Reservation are very dire. Per capita income is typically less than half of the U.S. average. Official unemployment rates are about four times of the United States.

The unofficial unemployment rate, including people not actively seeking jobs, as you've heard, is about six times the United States rate.

Family poverty and childhood poverty can be twice the average of the United States, and there are a couple of different mechanisms by we can all strive to overcome some of these dire economic conditions.

But first, as you know, is the Coal Production Tax Credit. Basic economics tells us that if tax credits are a way to decide a particular activity, one might consider the time horizon of the tax credit in conjunction with the activity that is going to be induced.

Obviously, coal mining is a long-term activity and, of course, a massive upfront investment. And so tax policy is aligned in terms of the time horizon. It simply makes more sense.

A permanent tax credit, or one that doesn't have to be renewed for decades, aligns itself much better with coal production than a temporary credit that is continually up for extension.

Secondly, as you know, uncertainty for coal produced on Indian lands, is the ability to access our markets. Basic economics tells us that any producer of any good, if they are seen liable for their product, basic potential for lower prices, greater risk, less investment in any production.

Given the infrastructure that we face here, and the topography and geography we're dealing with, that does in fact mean access to the Asian market, and I have some statistics about how the total coal demand in the United States is likely just to stay flat or decline slightly over the next several decades, while growing markets in Asia, China, India and South Korea may grow substantially.

Being able to access those markets would do wonders for the coal produced on Crow lands in terms of diversifying the consumer base and bring sustainable economic volume to the tribe.

And with that, I'd be happy to yield to the Committees.

[The prepared statement of Mr. Henson follows:]

PREPARED STATEMENT OF ERIC HENSON, SENIOR VICE PRESIDENT, COMPASS LEXECON; RESEARCH AFFILIATE, HARVARD PROJECT ON AMERICAN INDIAN ECONOMIC DEVELOPMENT

I would like to take a moment to thank you for the opportunity to visit the land of the Aps alooke and to speak today. My name is Eric Henson, and I am a Senior Vice President at Compass Lexecon, which is an economics consulting firm with offices located around the world.[1] I primarily work out of the Compass Lexecon offices in Boston, MA and Tucson, AZ. I also serve as a Research Affiliate with the Harvard Project on American Indian Economic Development,[2] and in that position I am engaged in an ongoing effort to understand what makes tribal economies work best.[3] I am a citizen of the Chickasaw Nation, and I grew up in one of the country's great oil producing regions, the Permian Basin of West Texas.[4]

I have a Master's Degree in Public Policy from the John F. Kennedy School of Government at Harvard University, an MA in Economics from Southern Methodist University, and a BBA in Business Economics from the University of Texas at San Antonio. I attended Harvard as the Kennedy School's Christian Johnson Native American Fellow. I have been engaged in Indian affairs since graduate school; my Master's thesis at Harvard examined the importance of a uniform commercial code for economic development on the Crow Reservation.[5] I've had the great privilege of visiting these tribal lands on several occasions.

The Harvard Project On American Indian Economic Development

Since its inception in 1987, the Harvard Project has collaborated with Native Nations to understand how and why tribal economies, social institutions, and political systems either succeed or fail. At the Harvard Project, my colleagues and I undertake research and teaching specifically tailored to meet the needs of tribal communities and tribal leadership.

One of the major questions the Harvard Project has been grappling with is: How is it that, despite widely-cited poverty and social distress, which is prevalent across numerous American Indian reservations, more and more tribes have been able to cast off the bonds of external economic dependence? We have seen more and more tribes taking part in what we have often referred to as an ''Indian Renaissance,'' where dynamic self-sustaining economies are created by tribal actions. These economies are built upon, and supported by, vibrant political and social institutions. The success stories are wide-ranging, from the property development and management of the Tulalip Tribes in Washington State, to sustained energy-based projects at Southern Ute, to the diverse array of professional and construction services offered by Ho Chunk, Inc. in Nebraska. Many tribes have begun actively challenging century-long economic paradigms and demonstrating effective self-determination and governance. It is curious that, contemporaneously, a number of other tribes experience continued economic hardship, high unemployment, rampant social and physical health challenges, and the like. What might be the causes of the striking economic and social divergences within Indian Country?

In the first years of HPAIED, the founding researchers recognized that what was needed in Indian Country was not additional unsolicited interference from outsiders, but culturally-specific educational programs and research, developed for tribes, and

---

[1] Compass Lexecon is an international economics consulting firm and is part of FTI Consulting.

[2] Referred to herein as ''HPAIED'' or ''Harvard Project.'' The Harvard Project is based at Harvard's John F. Kennedy School of Government in Cambridge, MA. We partner with the Native Nations Institute, which is located at the University of Arizona in Tucson, AZ. The Native Nations Institute provides executive education and leadership programs, uniquely tailored to senior executives and managers within the Native communities in Canada and the United States.

[3] See, e.g., The Harvard Project on American Indian Economic Development, *The State of the Native Nations: Conditions Under U.S. Policies of Self-Determination*, New York: Oxford University Press, 2008.

[4] I appear today not as a representative of Compass Lexecon or Harvard University. Furthermore, I have no financial interest in legislation that might impact tax rates applicable to coal production on Indian lands.

[5] A copy of my curriculum vitae has been retained in the Committee files.

undertaken hand-in-hand with tribal governments. The results of these studies are channeled back to those who must deal with the daily challenges of improving the economies and social conditions in Native communities (i.e., Indian people working in Indian Country).

In accordance with the above-mentioned approach, graduate students at the Kennedy School of Government and at the Native Nations Institute, working in close coordination with tribes; have completed several hundred projects and field research reports, many of which were on matters specifically requested by the tribes. These field projects have ranged from welfare reform at the Navajo Nation to bison ranching at Cheyenne River, and from judicial reform at Hualapai to ski resort management for the White Mountain Apache. As part of our organization's mission, many of these reports are available on our website for all tribes to learn from.[6]

Another important facet of the Harvard Project's work is our *Honoring Nations* program. *Honoring Nations* is a competitive awards program that identifies, celebrates, and shares outstanding success stories in tribal governance. We honor tribes that exemplify successful tribal governance, and to date the Harvard Project has recognized tribal governmental programs ranging from the Eastern Band of Cherokee for their Tribal Sanitation Program (in 1999) to the Effective Law Enforcement Program of the Gila River Police Department (in 2003) to the Seniors Skilled Nursing Facility at the Tohono O'odham Hospice (in 2008). Since 1999, we have honored nearly 120 tribal governmental initiatives.[7] HPAIED remains committed to empowering Native Nations through identifying the common characteristics of tribes that are successfully charting a course towards a socially, culturally, politically, and economically healthy future.

Research Findings

Prior to the 1980s, there was a notable lack of research pertaining to economic development in Indian Country. The small amount that was available contained at least two consistent themes: First, the overriding focus of thinking and policymaking was on what the Federal Government could do to create jobs, raise income, and increase household wealth. This helped contribute to the unbalanced relationship between the Bureau of Indian Affairs, other federal programs, and the tribes, which often became dependent on federal funding and expertise.

Second, the federal policies and programs that did exist within Indian Country constituted what we refer to as a ''Planner's Approach'' to economic and community development. The Planner's Approach was simplistic in treating economic development as a fundamental question of resources and expertise, as opposed to one of incentives and institutions. Viewing the world through the lens of the Planner's Approach, academics, government officials, and tribal leaders interpreted the underdevelopment seen on reservations as stemming from a lack of access to financial capital, technical skills, and managerial expertise. The Planner's Approach typically provided grants and loans in a well-intended effort to stimulate economic development. However, this heavy-handed approach was driven by federal budget allocations and has had a strong adverse impact on many Native communities. This approach created a world in which grant writers were always in short supply and tribal politics revolved around which elected officials could most effectively capture (or perhaps extract), funds from the federal government. Under the Planner's Approach, what was originally intended to be a solution to underdevelopment instead seems to have perpetuated it, degrading the core tenets of economic development into a series of rent-seeking behaviors.[8]

A fundamental flaw of the Planner's Approach was the erroneous assumption that a nation's economic development is a mechanical process that can be achieved by way of the imposition of a predetermined blueprint. While it is advisable and even advantageous to plan ahead, it is an exercise of hubris to think that one can ''plan'' an economy, in the sense of expecting tribal councils, national legislatures, or federal planners to correctly select a portfolio of businesses, projects, and activities that will not only survive, but will meet the needs of tribal citizens, and will thrive over time.[9]

---

[6] See the Harvard Project website at *http://www.hpaied.org/*.

[7] For more examples, see ''Honoring Nations: Directory of Honored Programs 1998–2010,'' *Honoring Nations Program,* The Harvard Project on American Indian Economic Development, at pages 9 and 11, at *http://hpaied.org/sites/default/files/documents/finalhndirectory.pdf.*

[8] ''Rent seeking'' is a term from economics and occurs when an organization or individual(s) seeks to obtain economic gain from others without reciprocating in the form of further wealth creation.

[9] Consider the natural experiment of the German economies after World War II. The parts of former Germany subjected to market forces (i.e., West Germany) became a powerhouse of de-

Continued

The discussion above raises one obvious question: If one cannot "plan" an economy to arrive at productive and sustainable development, what is the alternative? While there is no predetermined blueprint for success, there are some general tenets for effective, long-term economic development, and these tenets are now being demonstrated by a large number of tribes in Indian Country. We have found that these tenets of sustainable development are applicable to developing nations the world over, and are being acted upon by many successful tribes in Indian Country. A discussion of these tenets is found below, and in contrast to the Planner's Approach, we refer to tribes that are building their communities under these principles as governments engaged in a "Nation Building" process. [10]

Institutions Matter: The nature of a society's institutions, whether social, cultural, and/or governmental, determines the incentives around productive or unproductive activity. Within the scope of our research, the Harvard Project and the Native Nations Institute have consistently found that a tribe's economic development is anemic, or worse, unless the tribe's institutions personify at least three characteristics. The key attributes are:

- *A Rule of Law.* A respect for tribal law and the establishment of legitimate means for dispute resolution.

- *Separation of Politics from Day-to-Day Administration and Business Affairs.* Enterprises and economic transactions are free from societal politics and power struggles.

- *Efficient Bureaucracy.* Clarity of procedures, good record-keeping, efficient administration processes, reliable computer networks, and the like.

Culture Matters: Given the importance of institutions within a society, the social norms and worldview of the citizens that interact with those institutions also matter. [11] This lesson, observed repeatedly in our research with Native Nations, is an important tenet regarding economic development. The importance of local conditions and political willpower in building and promoting effective institutions as part of economic development cannot be understated. [12] Our research in Indian Country indicates that, for governing institutions to provide the foundation upon which sustained economic development can take place, there first must be a *cultural match.*

One can think of cultural match as the consonance between the structure of a society's formal institutions of governance (and its economic development initiatives) and its underlying norms of political power and authority (i.e., culture). [13] In order to function effectively, a society's institutions and corresponding economic development must be consistent with underlying cultural, political, and organizational norms. Simply put, they must be seen as legitimate in the eyes of the society's citizenry.

Sovereignty Matters: Self-determination is a key issue within Indian Country and its importance to economic development cannot be overlooked. There are four inseparable issues connecting sovereignty and self-determination to economic and community development within Indian Country. They are:

- *Design issues.* Without self-determination, it is impractical (and perhaps impossible) to change institutions so that they more closely match those of Native Nations and their unique economic needs.

- *Ownership issues.* Absent a strong sense of ownership, it is unquestionably difficult to get a local community involved and interested in how tribal economic investments pay off.

---

velopment in post-war Europe. The parts of the former Germany subjected to centralized planning (i.e., East Germany) stagnated and the citizenry had to be forcefully restrained from leaving for better opportunities elsewhere. For a discussion in the context of Indian Country, see, the Statement of Joseph P. Kalt, *Establishing a Tribal Development Corporation, Before the United States Senate Committee on Indian Affairs,* September 20, 2004 (hereinafter, "2004 Kalt Testimony"), noting that "Economic development is an organic process. In an environment in which opportunities are subject to the vicissitudes of competition and continually changing marketplace conditions, economic development occurs as the sum of small, adaptive decisions of myriad individuals who by luck or preparation are in the right place at the right time to take advantage of unplanned prospects. Economic development is much more analogous to tenacious plants looking for places to pop up and take root, than to an engineered system."

[10] For more information on the Nation Building approach, see: The Harvard Project on American Indian Economic Development, *The State of the Native Nations: Conditions Under U.S. Policies of Self-Determination,* New York: Oxford University Press, 2008, starting at page 26.

[11] Miriam Jorgensen, *Bringing the Background Forward: Evidence from Indian Country on the Social and Cultural Determinants of Economic Development,* Doctoral Dissertation, May 2000, at page 129.

[12] 2004 Kalt Testimony at page 13.

[13] 2004 Kalt Testimony at page 14.

- *Accountability issues.* Linked closely with the concept of ownership, those making the investments and program decisions need to be held accountable for how all federal (and tribal) resources are used.
- *Leadership development issues.* There are an increasing number of astute, capable, highly experienced leaders emerging within Indian Country. This is demonstrated by tribes (and tribal leadership) taking charge of issues irrespective of historical (or concurrently existing) federal support.

After years of research, it has become clear that tribes must have autonomy in order to foster institutions that are a cultural match for their societies. Successful tribal governments all exhibit effective institutions paired with a cultural match. We have come to believe that this is why policies of sovereignty and self-determination have been the only strategy that has shown any prospect of breaking the patterns of poverty and dependence that became so familiar on reservations from the late 1800s until at least the 1990s. It is only logical that it requires self-rule for a culture to put in place institutions that are a cultural match. Thus, we can restate the uniform qualities that have marked successful economic development in Indian Country as aggressive assertions of sovereignty, resulting in self-governed institutions that are characterized by a cultural match. It has repeatedly been shown that, when a tribe takes control of its own institutions and runs them in congruence with its own culture, the result is a set of economic, social, and political systems that work for its citizens.[14] Continued dependence on the federal government for grants and guidance removes accountability for tribal leadership and undermines the processes necessary for stable and lasting economic development. The negative results of such dependence should not be surprising.

The core tenets of Nation Building, which are required for effective economic development, are directly related to the issues that bring us here today. Over the past couple of decades, the Crow Nation has continued to push for increased autonomy and self-sufficiency and has made great strides in its efforts to build a sustainable economy. However, "the economic condition of the Crow is very poor. Jobs number few."[15] The Crow's efforts to play an active role in the regional economy by developing the tribe's abundant natural resources have brought jobs and revenue into the tribal economy, and have also benefited Big Horn County and the State of Montana. Similarly, proposals to maintain, and potentially expand, mining operations stand to substantially benefit the Crow Nation, the County, and the State. As noted by Chairman Old Coyote, "There are vast resources that can be developed to improve economic conditions of the Crow."[16] Harvard Project researchers, with support from the economics consulting firm where I work, recently undertook a study of coal mining on the Crow Reservation. Our study explicitly addressed the implications of continued/expanded mining for the Tribe, the County, and the State.[17] The complete study (has been retained in Committee files). I next summarize our findings and discuss the implications for economic development on the Crow Reservation.

Economic Development and Coal Mining on the Crow Reservation

Great progress towards sustainable economic development has been made on the Crow Reservation in recent years. However, efforts to revitalize the tribal economy began from such a low base (in terms of very low income levels, high poverty and unemployment rates, alarming health indicators, etc.) that much still needs to be done. Consider a few basic statistics, illustrated in Figures 1 and 2. As shown in Figure 1, between 2006 and 2010, the annual per-capita income of American Indians living on the Crow Reservation was $11,987 (compared to the U.S. average of $27,334; median household income showed a similar divergence). Figure 2 shows that during that same time period, when the national unemployment rate was ap-

[14] Stephen Cornell and Joseph P. Kalt, "Reloading the Dice: Improving the Chances for Economic Development on American Indian Reservations," *Joint Occasional Papers on Native Affairs,* No. 2003–02, 2003.

[15] Dennis Zotigh, "Darrin N. Old Coyote, Chairman: the Smithsonian National Museum of the American Indian's Meet Native America Series," October 31, 2013, at *http://blog.nmai.si.edu/main/2013/10/darrin-n-old-coyote-crow-nation.html.*

[16] Dennis Zotigh, "Darrin N. Old Coyote, Chairman: the Smithsonian National Museum of the American Indian's Meet Native America Series," October 31, 2013, at *http://blog.nmai.si.edu/main/2013/10/darrin-n-old-coyote-crow-nation.html.*

[17] Professor Joseph P. Kalt, *The Mining of Crow Nation Coal: Economic Impact on the Crow Reservation,* Big Horn County, and Montana, The Harvard Project on American Indian Economic Development, February 4, 2014 (hereinafter, "2014 Kalt Report").

proximately 8 percent, Crow unemployment hovered at about 32 percent. [18] Had we also included community members who had already given up searching for work, this unemployment rate would have been closer to 47 percent. [19] As noted above, per-capita income levels on the Crow Reservation are less than half that on the U.S. average, and family poverty levels reflect this same shortfall: During the five-year time period used in our recent study of coal development, the family poverty rate for the Crow Nation averaged 24 percent which was more than twice that of the average for the United States. Sadly, the poverty rate among Crow children during the study period was even more pronounced: Childhood poverty rates are alarming all across America, but on the Crow Reservation we saw a 39 percent rate (compared to the 19 percent rate for the United States). [20]

It is striking that such socio-economic conditions were (and are) present on the Crow Reservation, despite the tribe's abundance of valuable and accessible natural resources. These include "approximately 1.2 million acres of grazing land, 150,000 acres of dryland farmland, 30,000 acres of irrigated farmland," and of course a substantial reserve of coal, estimated at 17 billion short tons. [21] We are meeting here today to discuss coal development, and by any measure, the potential resource base of the Crow is impressive; the recoverable coal reserves in the Crow Nation account for nearly 12 percent of those in Montana and more than 3 percent of those of the U.S. as a whole. [22] These potential assets offer significant, unique, and potentially life-changing opportunities for individual Crow Indians and the entire Crow community. These opportunities should arise in the form of well-paying jobs, substantial royalty revenues to the tribe, and greater access to critical healthcare and social services, to name just a few. If the Crow Nation becomes unable to access these resources, then what is already a set of complex socio-economic challenges could easily degrade further.

As many already know, Westmoreland Coal Company has leased and operated the Absaloka Mine since the 1970s. The mine has been a significant part of the local economy ever since. In recent years, the Absaloka Mine alone has accounted for nearly two-thirds of the Crow Nation's non-federal budget; these are revenues that allow the tribe to pay for governmental salaries, provide social services, and to supplement federal funding to vital community programs such as Family Preservation, Tribal Elders, Head Start, and the Boys & Girls Club. [23]

---

[18] See, e.g., 2014 Kalt Report. According to the Montana Department of Labor & Industry, official unemployment on the Crow Reservation in 2012 was 25.1 percent (see Crow Nation, "Crow Reservation: Demographic and Economic Information," at page 6, October 2013, at *http://lmi.mt.gov/media/9409/rf13-crow-web.pdf*). This was still dramatically higher than the United States, which had an average unemployment rate of 8 percent throughout 2012 (see the U.S. Department of Labor, Bureau of Labor Statistics, "Labor Force Statistics from the Current Population Survey," 2012, at *http://data.bls.gov/timeseries/LNS14000000)*.

[19] Statement of Darrin Old Coyote, Chairman, Crow Nation, *Mining in America: Powder River Basin Coal Mining the Benefits and Challenges,* Before the House Committee on Natural Resources, Subcommittee on Energy and Mineral Resources, 113th Congress 2013 (hereinafter, "2013 Old Coyote Testimony"), at page 3.

[20] The U.S. Census, American Community Survey (ACS) 5-year data were presented because the U.S. Census typically provides the most complete and reliable data available. The ACS was utilized to ensure the accuracy and reliability of our study of coal development on the Crow Reservation. The ACS 5-year data for the years 2006–2010 were chosen because 2010 represents the last year that the necessary demographic information is available for American Indian or Alaskan Native residents on the Crow Reservation (and Off-Reservation Trust Land). More recent data (i.e., the ACS 5-year information for 2009–2013) show the combined demographic information of both American Indian or Alaskan Native residents and all other races residing in the area. According to these more recent data, combined unemployment on the Crow Reservation (and Off-Reservation Trust Land) was 29.2 percent, again dramatically higher than that of the U.S. as a whole (which was 9.7 percent). Family poverty rates were similarly divergent, 22.1 percent on the Crow Reservation and trust lands compared to 11.3 percent in the U.S. as a whole. As before, the child poverty rate on the Crow Reservation and trust lands was far too high, at 39.5 percent on the reservation, compared to 21.6 percent in the United States as a whole (see the U.S. Census Bureau, 2009–2013 5–Year American Community Survey, at *http://factfinder.* census.gov/faces/tableservices/jsf/pages/productview. xhtml?fpt=table).

[21] LAO Environmental, Inc., "Crow Indian Tribe: Resource Report," at pages 20 and 71, April 15, 2002, reported by the Bureau of Land Management, at *http://www.blm.gov/style/medialib/blm/mt/field* —*offices/miles\city/ogleis/crow.Par.79832.File.dat/minerals.pdf.*

[22] Montana's recoverable coal reserves are reported as 74.6 billion short tons and the total coal reserves in the United States are reported as 256.7 billion short tons (U.S. Energy Information Administration, "U.S. Coal Reserves with Data for 2012," December 16, 2013, at *www.eia.gov/coal/annual/pdf/table15.pdf).*

[23] Although the tribal budget is modest overall, services covered by the Crow Nation include important line items such as provision of supplemental money for staffing at the BIA-funded police department (see, e.g., Special Session of the Crow Tribal Legislature, *Approval of the Annual Budget for the Operation of the Crow Tribal Government and the Expenditure of Tribal*

Our 2014 study of coal on Crow lands evaluated the Absaloka Mine, and also assessed the potential economic value of the proposed Big Metal Project, an ongoing development initiative between the Crow Nation and Cloud Peak Energy (''Cloud Peak''). Our research found that in 2013, the average annual compensation and benefits for unionized Absaloka Mine workers exceeded $91,000 per person. [24] We found that expansion of operations at the Absaloka Mine, and/or initiation of mining at Cloud Peak's Big Metal Project, would be expected to create an impact of similar magnitude. [25] However, the benefits of such development do not accrue only to the specific workers with jobs in the mining industry. We must bear in mind that the economic impacts of mining operations on Crow lands extend far beyond just those to the local community. Big Horn County, the State of Montana, and the United States federal government also receive considerable economic benefits from coal produced on the Crow Reservation.

Our estimate is that the combined contribution of continued operation of the Absaloka Mine, along with the potential mining operations of the Big Metal Project, could contribute more than $370 million dollars annually to what is referred to as Gross Regional Product (GRP). [26] Annual state and federal tax revenues from the projects are estimated to be approximately $22.9 million and $21.9 million respectively. The government of the Crow Nation would likely benefit from as much as $107 million in royalties and taxes each year (see Figure 3) in addition to $3.75 million in initial option payments already received for the Big Metal Project. Such benefits, whether they be to the state, county, federal government, or tribal nation, could easily be lost if coal development and/or expansion at Crow is curtailed.

Research has noted that tribes that engage in the natural resource industries (such as the Crow Nation) are often overly and unjustly burdened by the current system. The Crow have been subjected to these burdens in multiple sectors of development. Consider, for a moment, an example from the oil and gas industry. In January 2005, the Crow Tribal Council approved an oil and gas lease on tribal lands, [27] but development of the resource was blocked until September 2007 due to the incomprehensibly slow review and approval process in place at the BIA. [28] Issues with the BIA persist: For example, the Crow Nation reports that BIA's records for surface and mineral ownership are repeatedly missing or out-of-date. [29] Bureaucratic inefficiencies, layers of regulatory oversight, near-complete lack of access to markets, higher-than-elsewhere permitting costs, and persistent infrastructure challenges create an environment of uncertainty and contribute to lackluster economic development. [30] In order to level the playing field for tribes, and allow them to overcome such hurdles to self-sufficiency, federal action can and should be taken at once.

One such action would be making the Indian Coal Production Tax Credit (ICPTC) permanent. Those present today know that the ICPTC assists mining firms in absorbing part of the production cost for coal operations on reservation land. The potential economic benefits of the tax credit include positioning of tribal coal so that

Revenue for Fiscal Year 2012, CLB 11–04, September 29, 2011, at http://www.crowlaws.org/trib-alllegislationl2002-present, at page 3).

[24] Salary and benefits data were provided for the 2014 Kalt Report by Westmoreland. The average annual salary for the unionized workforce at the Absaloka Mine was $56,264. Overtime and benefits, such as retirement funding and healthcare provision, brought the average annual compensation for all workers at the mine to $91,408.

[25] Due to its operation of the Absaloka Mine, employment opportunities with Westmoreland have been of great importance to the Crow Nation's citizens; roughly 70 percent of the mine's workforce is associated with the Crow Tribe (2013 Old Coyote Testimony at page 3). The mine typically employs on the order of 100 to 125 Crow Nation citizens or affiliated individuals (see, ''Daines introduces bipartisan legislation to encourage investment in Indian coal,'' *Sidney Herald,* June 7, 2014, and Statement of Scott Russell, Secretary, Crow Nation, *Tribal Development of Energy Resources and the Creation of Energy Jobs on Indian Lands, Before the House Committee on Natural Resources, Subcommittee on Indian and Alaska Native Affairs,* 112th Congress, April 1, 2011 (hereinafter, ''2011 Russell Testimony''), at page 11).

[26] GDP is defined by the U.S. Bureau of Economic Analysis as ''the market value of goods and services produced by labor and property in the United States.'' (See the BEA at *http://bea.gov/glossary/glossaryl*g.htm). GRP is similar to GDP, but it measures the total output of an economy within a specific region/area, rather than the national economy.

[27] Clair Johnson, ''Crow Tribe signs lease with oil exploration firm,'' *Billings Gazette,* May 16, 2005, *http://billingsgazette.com/news/state-and-regional/montana/crow-tribe-signs-lease-with-oil-exploration-firm/article85763605–8812–5993-a56d-8717f7c71bff.html.* See also, ''Crow Tribe Signs oil and gas development deal,'' May 17, 2005, *http://www.indianz.com/News/2005/008205.asp.*

[28] 2011 Russell Testimony at page 13.

[29] See, e.g., *On Improving Tribal-Corporate Relation in the Mining Sector: A White Paper on Strategies for Both Sides of the Table,* HPAIED, April 2014, at *http://hpaied.org/sites/default/files/documents/miningrelations.pdf,* at page 91.

[30] 2014 Kalt Report at page 2.

it is better able to compete in both national and international marketplaces. In addition, the tax credit provides an incentive which serves to promote expansion beyond current production levels on the Crow Reservation. However, this federal tax credit has heretofore been temporary, and has thus been consistently threatened. The temporary nature of this tax credit has contributed to instability in the limited number of tribal economies that rely on coal for their well-being. The uncertainty surrounding the tax regime applicable to coal production on tribal lands increases risk, and thus contributes to potential under-investment by mining firms operating within Indian Country (and, among those considering operations on tribal lands). Indeed, economics teaches that uncertainty around future tax rates can prevent firms from undertaking investments which cannot be reversed once they are made, and which pay off over long time horizons.

Although the ICPTC has (temporarily) provided a more level playing field for coal mining on the Crow Reservation, the tax credit alone is not sufficient to redress the bureaucratic impediments that stymie coal production on Native lands. An additional step that is critical for the Crow Nation to fully benefit from its coal resources would be securing equal access to expanded markets, both domestic and foreign.

Projected increases in international coal consumption highlights the importance of increasing access to foreign markets for coal produced on the Crow Reservation (as can be seen in Figure 4).[31] According to the U.S. Energy Information Administration, global consumption of coal is expected to increase from 147 quadrillion Btu in 2010 to 220 quadrillion Btu in 2040 (i.e., a 50 percent increase),[32] while domestic consumption is expected to remain relatively flat.[33] The disparity between the projected growth of global and domestic consumption emphasizes the importance of providing Native Nations access to international markets. However, the importance of access to international markets is not only derived from projected global demand growth. As with any product, providers need to mitigate the risks associated with having only a limited customer base.

The Crow Nation has recently suffered the consequences of only being able to access a limited market. In November 2011, the Sherburne County Generating Station (''Sherco'') in Becker, Minnesota, suffered a turbine malfunction which caused a fire in Unit 3. This fire shut the unit down for nearly two years.[34] The Absaloka Mine was specifically developed to supply coal to the Sherco plant.[35] The temporary shutdown of the plant resulted in a loss of approximately 50 percent of the Absaloka Mine's coal sales in 2012.[36] The drop-off in demand for coal produced on the Crow Reservation was followed by a curtailment of the workforce at the mine, which hurt individual tribal employees of the mine, the tribal government, and the community.[37] This loss clearly highlights the risk the tribe faces to its budget as a direct result of the Absaloka Mine's limited access to a wide range of potential buyers.[38]

The proposed Big Metal Project will exacerbate the need for access to international markets for coal produced on the Crow Reservation. In early 2013, Cloud

---

[31] U.S. Energy Information Administration, ''International Energy Outlook 2013,'' July 25, 2013, at *http://www. eia.gov/pressroom/presentations/sieminski*07252013.pdf, at page 6.

[32] U.S. Energy Information Administration, ''International Energy Outlook 2013,'' July 25, 2013, at *http://www. eia.gov/forecasts/ieo/pdf/0484(2013).pdf,* at page 67.

[33] U.S. Energy Information Administration, ''Annual Energy Report 2014: Early Release Overview,'' at *http://www.eia.gov/forecasts/aeo/er/pdf/0383er(2014).pdf,* at page 11. Consider the emerging economies of China and India. Coal consumption between those two countries has been projected to increase from 82 quadrillion Btu in 2010 to 144 quadrillion Btu in 2040, an increase of 76 percent. Compare this to the United States, which consumed 21 quadrillion Btu of coal in 2010 and is expected to remain at or below that level through 2040 (see Figure 5). The data cited here can be found at the U.S. Energy Information Administration, ''International Energy Outlook 2013,'' July 25, 2013, at *http://www. eia.gov/forecasts/ieo/pdf/0484(2013).pdf,* at pages 68–69 and 71.

[34] Elizabeth Dunbar, ''Xcel Energy Sherco plant returns to service after repairs,'' MPR News, October 21, 2013, at *http://www.mprnews.org/story/2013/10/21/environment/xcel-energy- sherco-plant-returns-to-service-after-repairs.*

[35] Tom Lutey, ''Soft Demand for Coal Ripples through Area Mines, Plants,'' Billings Gazette, June 24, 2012, *http://billingsgazette.com/news/state-and-regional/montana/soft-demand-for- coal-ripples-through-area-mines-plants/article*1ce7eb1fc-56e9–5a33-aa22–509c3f621ab9.html.

[36] Westmoreland Coal Company, FY 2011 Form 10K, at page 22.

[37] 2013 Old Coyote Testimony at page 3.

[38] There is also increasing pressure for the Absaloka Mine to supply a wider range of markets due to policy changes underway at Xcel Energy (''Xcel''). Xcel operates the Sherco Power Plant, and is one of the most important outlets for coal produced on the Crow Reservation. In January 2015, Xcel put forth plans to implement a reduction in coal-generated electricity at the Sherco plant (from 37 percent in 2015 to 29 percent in 2030), as part of an effort to transition to more renewable energy (see, e.g., David Shaffer, ''Xcel to Double down on Renewable Energy in Minnesota,'' *Star Tribune,* January 2, 2015, at *http://www. startribune.com/business/ 287387921.html).*

Peak announced an agreement with SSA Marine ("SSA") that provides an option to transport up to 17.6 million tons of coal through SSA's planned Gateway Pacific Terminal at Cherry Point ("Gateway Pacific"). [39] Completion of the Gateway Pacific facility is subject to obtaining the required permits and estimates for commencement of commercial operations appear to target a start date no earlier than 2018. [40] If completed, the Gateway Pacific facility would be the key export terminal to reach overseas markets for coal produced on the Crow Reservation, and basic economics tells us that a more diversified customer-base would mitigate the marketplace risks currently faced by those producing (or contemplating production of) coal on the Crow Reservation. [41] A level playing field for production on the Crow Reservation translates into more jobs for the citizens of the Crow Nation, with a number of benefits spilling over to Big Horn County and the State of Montana (e.g., increased tax revenues). [42] As noted above, the combined impact of continued production at the Absaloka Mine, along with operations getting underway at the Big Metal Project, is projected to be worth as much as $107 million in revenue to the Crow Nation's annual budget. This represents a four-fold increase in non-federal dollars currently available to the Crow government, and will markedly increase the tribe's ability to be self-sustaining and to provide for the needs of its citizenry.

Senator DAINES. Thank you for your testimony, Mr. Henson.

We are now going to move into some questions and answers.

Chairman Old Coyote and Speaker Bates, given the importance of coal to your people, I want to ask about the EPA's recognition of this when they developed their proposed clean power regulation. The EPA has stated they consulted with both the Crow and the Navajo Tribes during the formulation for this proposal.

At what stage did the EPA consult with your tribes, and was that consultation substantive? Did they take any action as a result of your concerns that you brought forward during this consultation? Chairman Old Coyote?

Mr. OLD COYOTE. We did receive a letter, kind of a general letter, kind of a "Dear Tribal Leader" letter. It didn't specifically talk about our resource or our coal mining or Crow people specifically.

And there's only three tribes in the whole United States that developed coal. Navajo, Hopi and Crow are the three tribes. And you

[39] Cloud Peak Energy, "2013 Annual Corporate Report," Gillette, WY, 2014, at page 3. Cherry Point is on the northern coast of Washington State in Whatcom County, just 17 miles south of the Canadian border and approximately 108 miles north of Seattle.

[40] Cloud Peak Energy, Press Release, "Cloud Peak Energy Announces Option Agreement with SSA Marine for Capacity at Future Cape Size Export Terminal in Pacific Northwest," February 13, 2013, *http://investor.cloudpeakenergy.com/press-release/business-development/cloud-peak-energy-announces-option-agreement-ssa-marine-capacity*. Current information indicates that final environmental impact statements are not going to be issued until 2017 (see, Washington State Department of Ecology, "Environmental Review: Gateway Pacific Terminal at Cherry Point Proposal," at *http://www.ecy.wa.gov/geographic/gatewaypacific/*). According to Cloud Peak, upon completion of the permitting process the Gateway Pacific facility must undergo two years of construction before it can begin operations, so prior indications of a 2018 start date are likely to slip back by more than a year.

[41] I note that the Gateway Pacific facility has stirred controversy, much of which involves the sovereign territory rights of the Lummi Nation of Washington State. The Lummi Nation asserts that Gateway Pacific infringes upon its ancestral fishing grounds, which are guaranteed by treaty. This is a delicate issue, and deserves respectful consideration by all parties involved. As discussed above, tribal sovereignty and autonomy are vital to economic growth and building well-functioning tribal communities, and these findings of the Harvard Project hold for all tribes (Crow, Lummi, and the hundreds of others found throughout Indian Country alike).

[42] Analysis provided by the House Committee on Ways & Means indicates the 10-year cost of the most recent one-year ICPTC extension is expected to be $38 million. This decrease in federal tax revenues is insignificant in the federal budget, so much so that USA Today has commented, "The budgetary cost of the Indian coal production credit is so small it doesn't show up in most Congressional Budget Office estimates." It is not surprising that a number of Montana's legislators have been working to make the ICPTC permanent (see, Gregory Korte, "In Montana, Crow Tribe sees perils to 'fiscal cliff'." See also, USA Today, November 19, 2012, at *http://www.usatoday.com/story/news/2012/11/18/crow-tribe-fiscal-cliff/1706695/*. Finally, see the United States House of Representatives, Committee on Ways & Means, "Section-by-Section Summary of HR 5771, The 'Tax Increase Prevention Act of 2014'," at *https://rules.house.gov/sites/republicans .rules.house.gov/files/113–2/PDF/113–HR5771–SxS.pdf*).

would think the EPA would come to all three tribes to consult on any kind of a coal issue where a coal policy that is going to be implemented, or the administration could move forward. So, no, there was no consultation.

We went back to D.C., spoke with the President directly. Mr. Bates and I were in the White House speaking with 12 other tribal leaders. And so Mr. Bates and I talked about the importance of coal. I talked about trying to diversify the use of coal.

And the next day, I was invited back to speak about the importance of coal to the Crow people. Invited back the third day. So the three days I spoke about coal to the President."

Finally, I was invited back a fourth time to talk about the effects it will have on the Crow people and so they never did mention or take into consideration the effect it would have on the Crow people if this EPA rule were to be implemented, today.

Senator DAINES. Thanks, Mr. Chairman.

Speaker Bates?

Mr. BATES. Thank you for the question.

That would depend on, Senator, at what level.

The first level is yes, they have consulted with the Navajo Nation to a certain extent.

To my understanding, there was negotiations; there were talks. And when I say at the lower level, I mean staff basically.

Senator DAINES. Were you ever involved in those consultations?

Mr. BATES. No.

Senator DAINES. Was the Department of the Interior ever involved in those conversations?

Mr. BATES. No.

The Department of Justice, as well as our environmental protection division were in consultations with the EPA but primarily staff.

And again, to my understanding, Senator, that those negotiations, they understood the impact of regulations as it pertained to the Navajo Nation in terms of revenue, in terms of jobs.

However, that conspiracy from the local level to the higher echelon of the Federal Government has not been taken into consideration.

So, you can look at it in two different ways.

Yes, but yet no at the end of the day, because whatever is decided as it pertains to Indian Country in terms of EPA regulations, isn't going to be done by the higher folks in Washington, D.C., and most likely, without consideration of the impact, in this case, to the Navajo Nation.

Senator DAINES. Thank you, Speaker Bates.

I want to turn to Attorney General Fox.

In a broader perspective, the EPA upholds obligations, you mentioned Executive Order 13175 in your testimony to, quote, "establish regular and meaningful consultations and collaboration with tribal officials in the development of Federal policies that have tribal implications."

What actions should the EPA have taken to be in compliance with that Order? In your view, what would regular and meaningful consultation look like if they were making an honest effort to comply with that Executive Order?

Mr. Fox. So, Senator Daines, first of all, let me reiterate, I don't believe that the EPA did meaningful consultation in a timely way with the three tribes that have coal production.

I think it's important to note, too, to distinguish that the "Dear Tribal Leader" letters, as the Chairman mentioned, were very generic. They didn't discuss or give a clue really about the impacts to any nation, tribal nation, if they have a coal resource. Instead, actually covered issues concerning tribal nations that may have a coal-fired generation plant on the reservation. Which of course, is not the case here.

And to be meaningful, I think the most important aspect of the Executive Order, it has to be consultation that's substantive, that engages the tribe, and that the EPA has done some work in advance to identify and determine which tribes may have specific circumstances for which consultation may be necessary rather than the blanket generic "Dear Tribal Leader" letter.

That has to be before the EPA presents, puts pen to paper, essentially, on the regulations. They need to consult with the tribes, and I believe come to tribal nations and meet with leadership. That didn't happen here.

I think it's also important to note that the Executive Order includes language that says where there are issues relating to tribal self-government or tribal trust resources, that the agency is to explore and use consensual mechanisms, including negotiated rulemaking.

And again, all of that needs to happen before the rules were even promulgated.

The last "Dear Tribal Leader" letter occured six days before the rules were promulgated. That's not meaningful, nor is it timely.

Senator DAINES. And to be clear, I personally called the EPA in Washington, D.C., and asked if they had members here, if Arizona and Boston could come be a part of this hearing, and hear the concern and also testify before this panel, and they declined to participate in the hearing.

Mr. Fox. Senator Daines, I also want to note for the record that I wrote personally to the administrator of the EPA asking them after they promulgated the rules to have a listening session here.

They had numerous listening sessions across the country. The nearest one was Denver. They declined to come here, which I think is also telling in terms of their responsiveness to our state's and the Crow Nation's concerns.

Senator DAINES. Thank you, Attorney General.

Speaker Bates, the EPA claimed it created an accommodation for coal plants across Indian County in the clean power regs.

While this is not going to help the Crow Tribe, because there's not a power plant here, but their buyers in Minnesota, which is subject to the EPA's plan, the Navajo Tribe does have a coal plants in their jurisdiction.

Does the EPA's claimed power plan in Indian Country address your tribe's concerns, and is it a workable plan?

Mr. BATES. No.

And I say this, again, with all due respect, Senator. In the testimony that I provided, I indicated the impact to the mining company in terms of jobs and revenue. That same scenario applies to the power plants.

As I indicated again, we had in the Four Corners Power Plant, five units. By virtue of the EPA, three of those units were shut down. Two are running as we speak. However, the retrofits that are required by virtue of the EPA standards, will have cost billions, and so that expense is going to be passed down to the customers, and it carries over into the mining company.

But, as we speak, production from our mine has been reduced significantly. So it does have a negative impact to the Navajo Nation in terms of revenue, in terms of jobs, in terms of stability of energy.

Senator DAINES. Thank you, Speaker Bates.

I want to shift gears here and talk about the Indian Coal Production Tax Credit discussed here in the testimony.

Chairman Old Coyote, what has been the effect of the expiration of the Indian Coal Production Tax Credit on the tribe's coal production, and how would extending that tax credit benefit the Crow Tribe?

Mr. OLD COYOTE. Well, first of all, the tax credit was established in 2006. The EPA set down a rule to close the Absaloka Mine down in 2006 because of the high sulfur content.

Then we went to the Senate, and we were told by the EPA to go to the Department of the Interior, they have welfare programs we could utilize if they shut down the mine. That was heat coming out of the EPA.

And so we went to Senator Baucus, then, who was the Chairman of the Finance Committee, and asked him to help us, and that's when he came up with the Indian Coal Production Tax Credit.

Three tribes, as I stated before, are mining coal, and it expired in 2012, extended for one year to 2013. But once that expired, we saw a $3 million to $4 million reduction in our budget.

Right now, the $4 million reduction in 2013 is starting to get into our budget where we're starting to do some furloughs and layoffs from the General Fund, and so the effects are real for Crow people.

You know, the unemployment rate is 47 percent, and with furloughs and some layoffs will come as a result of not having money from the Coal Production Tax Credit.

Moving forward, it would help level the playing field for our partners, Westmoreland, and for every ton of coal that is purchased by a company, that tax credit will level the playing field for all the bureaucratic red tape they have to go through just to mine a ton of coal.

And I should have brought that red tape with me that says all the bureaucratic red tape our partners have to go through just to mine a ton of coal.

And so all the money they spend, all the hurdles they have to go through just to mine on Indian land, this will level the playing field, and our coal will be favorable in the market, and we'll be independent of any intervention.

And so that's the benefit of going coal.

Senator DAINES. Many thanks, Mr. Chairman.

Mr. Henson, on December 1, 2014, the House Ways and Means Committee estimated that a one-year extension of the Indian Coal Production Tax Credit would cost $38 million for ten years.

Yet, your research has shown that the provision stimulates hundreds of millions of dollars in GDP.

The question for you, Mr. Henson, is, given the research and the economic impact to the Indian Coal Production Tax Credit on the economy growth of the Crow Tribe and the State of Montana, what sort of economic multiplier would you say this provision would have?

Mr. HENSON. The one slight caveat that I would throw out there to answer that question is the study combined the tax credit with the continued expanded production so we didn't separately parse out the impact of the tax credit versus the access to this wider marketplace.

The quick "off the cuff", employees at the Absaloka Mine, impacts of the daily cost is $38 million over ten years. That's about $4 million a year. Benefits just to the tribe alone is more than $100 million single representative year.

So, the tax credit being aligned with the mine production of this type of investment, along with this diversification and access to a broader set of customers is a 25:1 payoff.

Senator DAINES. So, conservatively you could parse that out, and it's still a very marginal multiplier?

Mr. HENSON. I would guess so, yes.

Senator DAINES. Regarding the permanency of the Indian Coal Production Tax Credit, if there's one thing I've learned during my relatively short tenure, serving in Washington, D.C., there's one thing Congress is good at, is creating uncertainty.

And the Indian Coal Production Tax Credit is yet another example that despite the economic needs, Congress seems to be sending mixed signals in its commitment to the Indian Coal Production Tax Credit, mixed signals to tribal communities, or if there are some incentives, it's only been on a short-term basis.

Mr. Henson, in terms of contract negotiations, business planning, what benefits would a permanent extension of this provision allow?

Mr. HENSON. Well, any investment in mining is a multi-year planning process. It's possible many hundreds of millions of dollars that you're asking an investor to make.

There are a handful of companies currently interested in actively negotiating or producing on those lands. So you have a willing set of parties, it's much better to have multi-year planning processes, investment processes, and production and overrun in the several decades.

So, as I said, it kind of aligns the time horizons with their investment.

If you live in a house 20 or 30 years, it's not really a coincidence that mortgages sort of align in terms of the time horizon you're looking at.

It is a similar analogy you might keep in mind here in terms of just aligning those incentives with the time horizon.

Senator DAINES. Thank you, Mr. Henson.

Attorney General Fox, you mentioned in your testimony in reference to coal exports, that Montana has a constitutional right to not have our interstate commerce unduly burdened by other states.

In your view, does that same right apply to tribes?

Mr. Fox. I believe it does.

The Commerce Clause in the United States Constitution, Article I, Section 8 Clause 3 specifically mentions tribes, and I think it's equally important that states, our sister states, be precluded from discriminating in commerce actions, and it's equally important to the Crow Nation and the Navajo Nation and other coal producing tribal nations as it is to individual states like Montana and Wyoming.

Senator Daines. Thanks, Attorney General Fox. A question to Chairman Old Coyote and Speaker Bates.

We talked about exports today. What impact would expanding a possibility coal export have on jobs for your tribes?

Start with Chairman Old Coyote.

Mr. Old Coyote. The positive impact for Crow people would result in more jobs and more revenue.

The Army Corps of Engineers is doing a study on that, the lead agency on that, so that would have a real positive impact on the Crow people to be another source of revenue, and there would be more jobs for the Crow people.

Right now, with just one mine and it is like one egg in the basket, and the EPA looking down at the Crow people for their coal.

I think another source of revenue would help the Crow people move forward to a better, brighter future.

Senator Daines. Thanks, Mr. Chairman.

Speaker Bates.

Mr. Bates. Thank you, sir.

As I indicated in my testimony, our production right now is from 8 to 10 million tons down from 13 to 16 million. That's significant in terms of, jobs.

When you look at the jobs that are required from 13 to 16 million tons, we have less jobs as we speak today.

So, by being able to export, the jobs will return, and the revenue will return. It would have a positive impact, Senator, if the nation was to go to exports.

Senator Daines. Thank you, Speaker Bates.

I want to shift gears here, Mr. Henson. I've heard arguments that the Crow Tribe, the Navajo, the state of Montana and Wyoming should leave the coal in the ground due to concerns about climate change. In fact, it is one of the driving arguments against exporting Crow and Montana coal in the Asian markets.

The Gateway Pacific Terminal that was discussed here today. Its projection was about 48 million tons of coal per year, almost all of it will come from Montana, the Crow, and the state of Wyoming.

It's my understanding that there's a growing demand for energy in Asia, and Montana Powder River Basin coal is cleaner coal. Why not allow cleaner coal to meet global energy demands? What are the impacts on that amount of coal on climate change and the Asian market?

Mr. Henson. That question brings a few thoughts to mind. One is, we should keep in mind no one really wants a lump of coal for a gallon of gasoline. People want heating for their homes or in their offices.

So, the progress that people really demand in Asia are energy for a myriad of uses. And there are 2 billion people in India and China only who are, for the most part, growing into a middle class society, and those people are going to need a massive amount of energy to stay on that path.

I kind of looked into the statistics for China, India, Japan and South Korea. In a single year, those four nations consume about 5 billion tons of coal. So the amount that was cited here, the 48 million, is less than 1 percent of that.

Senator DAINES. So 48 millions tons of coal coming out of coal country here versus 5 billion tons.

Mr. HENSON. For just four countries.

It's a very small amount. During the course of our study, the numbers that we saw for Crow coal amounted to like 3/10th of 1 percent.

Senator DAINES. So, to shift gears on coal production from Montana, even off the reservation, Attorney General Fox, how does the Asian coal and India demand affect the state of Montana off the reservation?

Mr. FOX. Senator Daines, let me first say, the members of the Crow Nation are Montanans. They are Americas. Anything that affects them affects all of us. It affects me, and it affects you, and we need to keep that in mind.

Certainly Crow coal, when it's mined, doesn't provide severance taxes in particular to the state of Montana. Obviously Powder River coal does, but Crow coal doesn't provide taxes directly to the state.

But as has been mentioned today, it provides a huge economic impact to not only this corner of the state, but the entire state. There's jobs, retail purchasing that goes on, and all the things that are basically an economic ripple effect, and so this is very important to Montana.

It's important to our state officials. I know there are representatives from the Governor's office here who are very invested in this issue.

And I want to thank Jason Smith, who is the Governor's tribal liaison, for being here, because I know that we discuss these issues with them quite a bit.

We want to make sure that the economic impacts are not lost in this discussion, as the Chairman said, it affects real people right here in this area, and those are the people I'm most concerned about. This is my home.

Senator DAINES. Thanks, Attorney General Fox.

Mr. Small, if the coal industry suffers a decline in this area, what jobs would be available for boilermakers or other union members that currently work in the coal industry?

Mr. SMALL. Well, you know, I'm really not aware of any, or at least nothing that can bring the financial stability to the good-paying jobs that the coal industry brings to this area.

Senator DAINES. So, are there industries in the area that you can think of that can absorb these people, or are they going to have to leave the area to find a job?

Mr. SMALL. Well, I'm sure they'll probably be a few jobs around which are a lot lower paying and stuff.

And again, we'll flood the market with competent people that could be doing other things, and I'm sure a lot of them will have to leave the area.

Senator DAINES. Mr. Small, will coal development in Indian Country be compatible with traditional native values in the close relationship with the land?

Mr. SMALL. Oh, absolutely.

I would think the Navajo and the Crow constituency in this room right now can attest to that. They can, and it is happening already.

I would believe that any tribes that are wanting to develop, if they had concerns they should be able to negotiate agreements and also create economic growth.

Senator DAINES. Chairman Old Coyote and Speaker Bates, similarly, how would you characterize the relationship between coal production and environmental stewardship?

Chairman Old Coyote?

Mr. OLD COYOTE. In our experience out at the Absaloka Mine, you know, if you haven't been out there, we invite people to go and see where the open pit mine was before and then after.

Right now in some of the areas, all the reclamation work that's done is better than what it was before.

And, you know, a lot of people don't think that way. They have this mentality or mind set that with an open pit, there's dirty coal everywhere.

But once you go out there and see the reclamation work—and the people that did the reclamation are tribal members, and so they take great pride in doing good work, getting the coal out.

In the next couple of days here, all the crews that did labor, every tribal member will receive payment from that coal mine.

And so, you know, they take great pride not only taking the coal out, but also restoring it back to better than what it was, and that is what our Crow people are doing.

Senator DAINES. Speaker Bates.

Mr. BATES. Just to reiterate what the Chairman indicated, in the Navajo Nation it's a similar situation when it comes to Mother Earth. We are very dear to and will protect Mother Earth in whatever is needed to move the Nation forward.

And as the Chairman indicated, our own Navajo people who are within the reclamation division of our coal mine, take great pride in bringing those lands back to where they can be used for future generations.

Senator DAINES. Thanks you, Speaker Bates.

Last question. I've heard concerns as I travel around Montana about the impacts of coal dust from coal traveling by train across towns in Montana.

Chairman Old Coyote, you talked about what goes on now on these coal trains and so forth. Should Montanans be concerned about coal dust traveling from rail shipments of Montana coal to West Coast terminals?

Mr. OLD COYOTE. No, we've never had a problem with coal dust here. As long as I can remember, the coal has been traveling through the reservation.

I know for years nobody has ever had a problem with coal dust until—the only time we started hearing about coal dust was after the Gateway Pacific Terminal was announced, and NGOs started making a issue about coal dust. But before that, there was no complaints.

For the last few years, our coal has been going to the Midwest, and just recently to the Washington power plant. And the coal has been traveling that railroad for years, and there's never been a problem.

Now they're claiming that the coal dust is going to be a problem. But it's NGOs that are making this claim, you know, regardless of what the NGOs say, Crow people are going to continue mining coal, because unless they have an alternative to feed my people, to help my people go forward, we're going to continue to mine coal.

Senator DAINES. There's an old saying, "You're entitled to your own opinion, but you're not entitled to your own facts."

I'm also proud of the fact that it was Montana coal that powered all those Detroit-Edison power plants out in the Midwest that actually powered the U.S. Bonnefield Manufacturing Industry—Montana coal.

Well, if there are no more comments for today, members of the Committee may also submit written questions for the record, and the hearing record will be open for two weeks.

The Montana Chamber of Commerce along with Governor Bullock and Senator Tester have also submitted testimony which will be included in the official record.

I want to thank the witnesses for their time and testimony today and look forward to bringing these comments back to Congress with me as I get back next week.

You know, we've got a lot of work to do to convince folks back there that coal is an essential part of our energy portfolio. It is the life blood of the economy in a number of parts of the country, including right here on the Crow Reservation.

While we heard about the devastating effects the EPA's clean energy regulations would have on our economy, we also heard about some concrete steps we can take to ensure the stability of the coal industry in Indian County.

Making the Indian Coal Production Tax Credit permanent ought to be an important first step, alongside using Northwest ports to ship our coal overseas, adding new consumers for our product, and allowing tribes to get a fair market value for their coal.

With that, the hearing is adjourned.

[Whereupon, at 12:15 p.m., the hearing was concluded.]

APPENDIX

PREPARED STATEMENT OF HON. JON TESTER, U.S. SENATOR FROM MONTANA

I would like to thank Chairman Barrasso for scheduling this field hearing in Crow country, Montana. I would also like to thank the Crow Tribe for their generous hospitality in hosting this special field hearing.

It's important that this Committee continue to look closely at the various forms of economic development occurring in Indian County. As we all know, each tribal nation is unique, and every reservation or tribal community has specific resources available for development.

The ability for tribes to successfully and responsibly manage their natural resources, while building self-determination, is crucial for the economic success of Indian Country. I'm glad the Senate Committee on Indian Affairs acknowledges these efforts on behalf of tribes, and has taken a specific interest in the innovative means of economic development that are happening in the Crow Nation. I think it's clear that the future of Crow is in energy, and responsible development of their resources will benefit the Tribe, the state of Montana, and the country as a whole.

From the time I became a United States Senator in 2006, until today, Crow leaders have stressed the importance of the Indian Coal Production Tax Credit to their people, in promoting self-sufficiency, creating and sustaining jobs, and building a stable base for economic development. I have heard the Tribe loud and clear, and I have fought for the continuation of this critical tax credit with each passing year. I know how important this resource is to the Crow Nation, and I will continue to advocate for the credit in Washington.

The Tribe has worked to develop its coal resources for years. They are now showing bold leadership by venturing into new markets and diversifying their energy portfolio. I applaud these efforts to ensure a strong future for Crow children and grandchildren.

One example of this innovation is the recently announced partnership between the Department of Interior and the Crow Nation to enter into an agreement for hydropower development. The Yellowtail Dam project stems from the historic Crow Tribe Water Rights Settlement Act of 2010. Former Senator Baucus and I worked with the Tribe to ensure the hydropower provisions were included in our final legislation. Under this important law, the Crow Tribe has the exclusive right to develop and market power generation on the Yellowtail Afterbay Dam. This agreement will create jobs and a more energy independent future for families here in Crow Nation.

Crow is showing the smart innovation that will help other tribes throughout Indian Country realize the potential in their own lands, and move towards self-determination. I look forward to the testimony of the witnesses today, and in seeing how the Committee can help propel economic development for all tribes even further.

PREPARED STATEMENT OF HON. STEVE BULLOCK, GOVERNOR, STATE OF MONTANA

Dear Chairman Barrasso and Members of the Senate Committee on Indian Affairs:

Thank you for the invitation to attend the Oversight Field Hearing on economic self-determination in Indian Country, provided to my office late last week. I am unable to attend as I have had a long-standing commitment to visit the Signal Peak Coal Mine, to observe first-hand its operations and to meet with management and employees. As a member of Montana's Land Board, I have been a strong supporter of the mine.

Coal continues to be an important source of economic opportunity and jobs for Crow Country, and I will continue to support the Tribe's efforts to develop their resources. I am also confident that the Crow can lead the way in responsible coal development in Indian Country. I also congratulate the Northern Cheyenne as they were finally successful late last year in passing federal legislation to restore long overdue mineral rights, giving them access and the option to develop coal on their land.

Improving the economic health of the sovereign Indian Nations within Montana's borders continues to be a focus of my administration. The Main Street Montana in Indian Country initiative seeks to strengthen state-tribal partnerships to develop infrastructure, increase access to capital, and promote economic growth.

Economic self-determination requires a strong cultural and educational foundation, and we have also prioritized our commitment to the Montana Indian Language Preservation Pilot Program and other innovative approaches to improving education in Indian Country.

In addition, a healthy economy depends upon clean water and air. Montanans know the climate is changing—we're outdoors people and we see it happening before our eyes. We also need reliable low-cost electricity to power our homes and businesses, and support economic growth. It's clear to me that this is not an either/or scenario, as some would lead us to believe.

We can meet the challenges posed by climate change and create good-paying jobs and a more vibrant economy. That includes within the sovereign Indian Nations—whether it's coal or hydropower on the Crow Reservation, hydropower on the Flathead Reservation, or harnessing wind power which is an opportunity that exists across Indian Country.

Coal is an important part of our future—it's abundant and accessible. As with other fuels, even natural gas, the success of coal will require significant public investment and broad public support.

I feel strongly that Washington DC has not done enough to advance clean coal technologies. Instead, the debate there is often about whether someone is a "climate change denier" or if the President is waging a "war on coal," with lawyers and lobbyists leading the charge.

Meanwhile, increasing energy demand—both domestic and international—is charting our future course, and we'll need both carbon-based and renewable sources of energy in the coming decades. I'm proud that Montana is leading the way in much of the clean energy research being done in this country. These emerging technologies being pioneered on our university and college campuses—including low-carbon coal research—will pave the way to a cleaner energy future and the good-paying jobs that come with it. Unfortunately, as a country, we have not prioritized this research enough.

Climate change is a global issue, and the United States will play an important role in any solution. We should lead, and also recognize that we can't solve this issue on our own. With global demand for energy forecast to grow, coal is likely to continue to be an important resource for other nations as well. I have great respect for the power of any state to address policy challenges and meet the needs of its citizens as it sees fit. However, I am very concerned when one state takes action that could have significant economic consequences for Montana. This is especially true for an issue like climate change, where action on a much larger scale will be necessary to be successful.

As the executive of the state, I must protect Montana's interests and follow the law. Last December I expressed in writing my concerns with the President's Clean Power Plan. In my comments to the proposed rule I requested changes to both protect Montana's coal industry and strengthen the state's hand in facilitating new economic opportunities and jobs for Montanans through renewable energy and energy efficiency.

I thank the Senate Indian Affairs Committee for coming to Crow and holding this hearing. It is important that we maintain positive government to government cooperation as the United States, Montana and tribal nations continue to responsibly develop our natural resources.

The promise is in the future. What we know today will be eclipsed by tomorrow—whether it's the challenge of integrating wind power and other renewables or the carbon emissions associated with coal. We simply won't get to a low carbon and secure energy future without vision and commitment, grounded in today but unafraid of tomorrow.

PREPARED STATEMENT OF THE NAVAJO NATION

Elsa Johnson, from Black Mesa and Director of Iina Solutions: Even after 50 years, coal mining has not made Navajo rich. We contend with contamination, pollution, water depletion, and toxic ponds. Plus our poverty and high unemployment still hasn't improved. And, most of our people are still hauling water and live without electricity!

Adella Begaye, nurse and member of Dine CARE: I understand the old 4 corners mine that Navajo Nation bought for 80 million and thought they would generate funds was a mistake, (we told them). Now it is in the red for 130 million, coal is being phased out and they cannot even sell the coal at a fair price. So Mr. Bates as one of the sponsors pushing to buy a mine is now going defunct and we are also liable for 100 million tons of coal ash.

Percy Deal, former Council Delegate, resident of Black Mesa, board member of Dine CARE and To Nizhoni Ani: My comment is: (1) These giant industries that moved onto the Navajo reservations over 60 years ago in the four corners and Black Mesa have not brought any job multiplier on to the reservation. The jobs are the direct jobs, and they are now declining. All businesses that happened over those years are located off reservation, not a single one on reservation. (2) These industries are controlling the minds of Navajo leadership making them believe there is no way we could survive without them, they bring jobs and revenues. As results our leadership are all in a capsule believing it and that there is no other way. (3) Lorenzo Bates led the Council to believe that buying the Navajo mine is the best investment, but things are changing now. The Nation is looking for someone to buy their coal, there are damages left behind that the federal court is ordering cleaned-up and Navajo Nation is left holding that bag. NTEC (Navajo Transitional Energy Company) will soon be coming to the Navajo Nation asking for approximately $45M. (4) Water and air are contaminated which will have to be clean up. (5) Self-Determination on Navajo? Bates and LT are at the verge of dismantling a third of the Navajo government. Should that happen, no businesses or government will want to come in because of the destruction of the Judicial branch.

These individuals and others also pointed to the recent video "Cursed by Coal: Mining the Navajo Nation" by Vice News: *https://m.youtube.com/ watch?v=F4uGCj6knVw&feature=youtu.be.* The video lays out significant environmental, health, Navajo population displacement, and quality of life problems associated with coal development on Navajo Nation.

PREPARED STATEMENT OF ALAINA BUFFALO SPIRIT, ENROLLED MEMBER, NORTHERN CHEYENNE TRIBE; MEMBER, NORTHERN PLAINS RESOURCE COUNCIL

Chairman Barrasso and Senators of the Indian Affairs Committee,

My name is Alaina Buffalo Spirit. I am an enrolled member of the Northern Cheyenne tribe and a landowner near Birney on the southern end of the Northern Cheyenne Reservation. I am also a member of Northern Plains Resource Council.

Thank you for allowing me to submit my perspective on coal development in Indian Country today. Today's Field Hearing has a small number of hand-picked witnesses. I am afraid those witnesses will not truly represent the will of Native peoples, and especially the will of my people, the Northern Cheyenne. In particular, I would like to emphasize that Jason Small does not speak officially for the Northern Cheyenne.

It is true that the Northern Cheyenne have a weak economy right now, and it is true that we need to work to build a stronger, more resilient economy. But coal cannot bring prosperity, and it will harm our people.

The 57 Affiliated Tribes of Northwest Indians passed a resolution in 2012 stating that they oppose export of coal from Montana and Wyoming through the Pacific Northwest. The Lummi have formally asked that the government reject the permit to construct the Gateway Pacific Terminal because it would violate their treaty rights, disrupt their economy, and damage sacred lands. The Northern Cheyenne people have never said they want coal to come to their reservation. We are surrounded by coal mines and coal plants, and have seen only a worsened economy and destruction of our homeland.

For the record, I am submitting with my testimony two guest editorials published in the Billings Gazette last Saturday, April 4, 2015 (retained in Committee files— see website addresses below), as well as the resolution of the 57 Affiliated Tribes of Northwest Indians and a letter from the Lummi Nation Business Council to the Army Corps of Engineers requesting that the Cherry Point terminal not be constructed.

http://billingsgazette.com/news/opinion/guest/guest-opinion -northern-cheyenne-future-is-in-sun-wind/article\178e86ca-d024–5802–8353– 7b2304fe05e3.html

http://billingsgazette.com/news/opinion/guest/guest-opinion -coal-mining-fails-to-bring-prosperity-to-reservations/article\22275946–0704–5bab- 9c50-eb4ebb515c2e.html

LETTER, DATED JAN. 5, 2015 TO COL. JOHN G. BUCK, SEATTLE DISTRICT COMMANDER, U.S. ARMY CORPS OF ENGINEERS, FROM TIM BALLEW II, CHAIR, LUMMI INDIAN BUSINESS COUNCIL

SUBJECT: Lummi Nation Request for Denial of Permit for the Proposed Gateway Pacific Terminal Bulk Dry Goods Shipping Facility (Ref. No. NWS–2008–260).

Colonel Buck:

The Lummi Nation is opposed to the Gateway Pacific Terminal (Ref. No. NWS–2008–260) project proposed at Xwe'chi'eXen (Cherry Point). (See attached resolution). We are requesting that the U. S. Army Corps of Engineers (Corps) take immediate action and deny the permit application based, *inter alia,* on the project's adverse impact on the treaty rights of the Lummi Nation. The impacts on the Nation's treaty rights associated with this project cannot be mitigated.

The waters and tidelands impacted by this project are an integral part of the usual and accustomed fishing places of the Lummi Nation. *United States v. Washington,* 384 F. Supp. 312, 360–61 (W.D. Wash. 1974), aff'd, 520 F.2d 676 (9th Cir. 1975), cert. denied, 423 U.S. 1086 (1976); see also, *United States v. Washington,* 873 F.Supp., 1422 (W.D. Wash. 1994), *aff'd in relevant part,* 157 F.3d 630, 643–644, 646–47 (9th Cir. 1998). As part of the permitting process for this project, the Corps is required to ensure that the Nation's treaty rights are not abrogated or impinged upon. *Northwest Sea Farms v. United States Army Corps of Engineers,* 931 F. Supp. 1515 (W.D. Wash. 1996).

Review of the impacts associated with this project, including, but not limited to, those analyzed in the *Gateway Paddle Terminal Vessel Traffic and Risk Assessment Study* lead to the inescapable conclusion that the proposed project will directly result in the substantial impairment of the treaty rights of the Lummi Nation throughout the Nations' "usual and accustomed" fishing areas. (See attached sections). The Lummi have harvested at this location since time immemorial and plan to continue into the future. The proposed project will impact this significant treaty harvesting location and will significantly limit the ability of tribal members to exercise their treaty rights. (See attached declarations).

Additionally, the Lummi Nation has a sacred obligation to protect Xwe'chi'eXen based on the area's cultural and spiritual significance. The Corps is obligated to comply with the mandates of the National Historic Preservation Act, specifically section 106, in evaluating the project's potential impacts. This obligation is in addition to the Corps' obligations that spring from our treaty rights. The Lummi Nation is opposed to this project due to the cultural and spiritual significance of Xwe'chi'eXen, and intends to use all means necessary to protect it.

In addition to the proposed project's unacceptable and unavoidable impacts to the Nation's access to this significant treaty harvesting location, and to the cultural integrity of the site, the proposed project location is within an especially rich and fertile marine environment that serves as important habitat for a number of forage fish, finfish, and shellfish (including several threatened and/or endangered species) that are inextricably linked to the Lummi *Schelangen* ("Way of Life"). Anticipated impacts to this significant aquatic environment include, but are not limited to, substantially increased ballast water discharges and associated risk of introducing invasive species, contaminant spills (product, bunker fuel oil, crude oil and refined products from adjacent facilities), noise, and vessel traffic. The impacts to these critical marine waters from coal alone may include: smothering, toxicity, substrate change, accumulation, and water quality degradation.

The devastating environmental impacts associated with this project, as well as the trust responsibility of federal agencies to ensure the protection of the treaty rights of the Lummi Nation, mandate the denial of any and all permits under the Corp's jurisdiction.

RESOLUTION #13-47—OPPOSE THE PROPOSALS FOR THE TRANSPORTATION AND EXPORT OF FOSSIL FUELS IN THE PACIFIC NORTHWEST

PREAMBLE

We the members of the Affiliated Tribes of Northwest Indians of the United States, invoking the divine blessing of the Creator upon our efforts and purposes, in order to preserve for ourselves and our descendants rights secured under Indian Treaties, Executive Orders, and benefits to which we are entitled under the laws and Constitution of the United States and several states, to enlighten the public toward a better understanding of the Indian people, to preserve Indian cultural values, and otherwise to promote the welfare of the Indian people, do hereby establish and submit the following resolution:

WHEREAS, the Affiliated Tribes of Northwest Indians (ATNI) are representatives of and advocates for national, regional, and specific tribal concerns; and

WHEREAS, ATNI is a regional organization comprised of American Indians/Alaska Natives and tribes in the states of Washington, Idaho, Oregon, Montana, Nevada, Northern California, and Alaska; and

WHEREAS, the health, safety, welfare, education, economic and employment opportunity, and preservation of cultural and natural resources are primary goals and objectives of the ATNI; and

WHEREAS, since time immemorial, our economy, culture, religion and way of life has centered around our fishing, hunting and gathering resources, and the lands and waters on which they depend, and we have been, and remain, careful and conscientious stewards over them to ensure their continued health and well-being; and

WHEREAS, the tribes of ATNI depend on the natural resources of this region to sustain our way of life, rights to fish, hunt and gather, our economies, human health and fulfill our sacred obligation to protect our First Foods and our most precious natural resource, water; and

WHEREAS, the tribes of ATNI have previously adopted Resolution No 12–53, in September 2012, recognizing the potential impacts of coal export terminal proposals that have come to the Northwest and the action directed to the Army Corp of Engineers to conduct a full regional Environmental Impact Statement (EIS) to address the significant cumulative impacts of these proposals, and

WHEREAS, the Northwest is facing the advancement of more fossil fuel exports, including numerous oil-rail proposals in Oregon and Washington, which would bring 500,000 barrels of oil a day via rail line to and across Northwest waterways as well as expansion of pipeline capacity from Alberta to British Columbia and Washington State, and

WHEREAS, based on review of proposals at these sites these past twelve months, the tribes of ATNI believe these energy transportation and export proposals will diminish our salmon habitat, our fishing, hunting and gathering rights, our treaty, indigenous, and inherent rights and resources, our life way, and will destroy sacred places of the Pacific Northwest tribes; and

WHEREAS, the tribes of ATNI respect and honor our Sacred Places just as we do our natural resources, including the Lummi Sacred Site known as Xwe'Chi 'eXen where our ancestors are at rest, and the sacred traditional reef net sites at Cherry Point, Washington; and therefore call upon agencies to fulfill their statutory and legal responsibility to fully comply with Section 106 of the Historic Preservation Act; and

WHEREAS, the Northwest Tribes' ancestral industry of fisheries relies on sustainable resources that will face detrimental impacts from the transportation and export of nonrenewable fossil fuel resources; now

THEREFORE BE IT RESOLVED, that ATNI is in opposition of the transportation and export of fossil energy in the Northwest based on infringement and endangerment upon indigenous, inherent, and treaty-protected resources, impacts on human health, economies, sacred places and our traditional way of life, and

BE IT FURTHER RESOLVED, the tribes of ATNI support a strategy to document the impacts of these fossil fuel energy transport and export proposals, which includes baseline studies of science from a local approach, impacts to the economies, as well as legal and policy initiatives.

CERTIFICATION

The foregoing resolution was adopted at the 2013 Mid-Year Convention of the Affiliated Tribes of Northwest Indians, held at the Northern Quest Resort and Casino, Airway Heights, Washington ton on May 13–May 16, 2013 with a quorum present.

www.ingramcontent.com/pod-product-compliance
Lightning Source LLC
Chambersburg PA
CBHW081116280526
45787CB00007B/2853